3 Wise Teachers

General Inquiries (919) 391-8180 or visit us at www.3WiseTeachers.com.

THE ONLY
×
THING
IN LIFE
ACHIEVED WITHOUT
EFFORT IS
×
FAILURE

Table of Contents

EXAMINATION CONTENT OUTLINE
FOR NORTH CAROLINA REAL ESTATE LICENSING EXAMINATION

The exam consists of 40 scored State questions. You may also be given up to 5 additional questions that are being evaluated for possible future exam use. You will not know if you are answering a scored test question or a question that is being evaluated for possible future use, or which ones will count towards your final grade. **To receive a passing score, you must answer 29 out of the 40 graded State questions correctly.** You may use a hand-held battery operated calculator that does not have programable capabilities on the exam.

You will have 2 hours to take the State portion of the test.

Examination Content Outline – State 40 Scored Questions:

A. North Carolina Commission Rules and License Law	24 Questions
B. Other North Carolina Laws and Practices	11 Questions
C. General Real Estate Topics	5 Questions

For additional details about these topics see Real Estate Licensing in North Carolina published by the North Carolina Real Estate Commission (see pages 20-22). It is highly recommended that you review License Law and Commission Rule Comments (see page 39 of this workbook), as 24 out of the 40 questions that you will be required to answer will come from this document.

IMPORTANT TIPS AND SUGGESTIONS

The examination is a standardized test and therefore you should never leave a question blank. Make sure to read all answer choices carefully and note "yes", "no" or "maybe" on your scratch paper. Remember if you can eliminate 2 wrong answers you have a 50/50 chance of selecting the correct answer. You can skip a question and return to it later if you are not sure how to answer, but be sure you make note of the question you are skipping so that you do not miss scoring your answer. Be careful when a question makes a definitive statement (always, never, must or shall), as these are often distractors. Shall is a polite way of saying must. If you are unsure of how to answer a math problem, if possible, try to work the problem backwards by using the answers provided. It is recommended that you start with answer choice "C" and then determine if the answer needs to be higher or lower.

In preparation for the examination you need to study and **memorize** all KEY facts outlined in this workbook. Important topics which have a ⚠ symbol will be heavily tested and must be memorized.

North Carolina Real Estate License Law and Commission Rules (24 Questions) – It is highly recommended that you review License Law and Commission Rule Comments in preparation for the exam.

2 QUESTIONS] – Activities requiring a license, exempt activities, requirements to obtain a license and activities of unlicensed assistants

- ○ When do I need to be a licensed Real Estate Broker?
  - ➢ **LLBEANS** – When someone Lists, Leases, Buys, Exchanges, Auctions, Negotiates or Sells real property **for another, for compensation**.
  - ➢ An active real estate license that is in good standing is required to advertise and conduct an auction of real estate, however the mere crier of sale is not required to hold a real estate license.
  - ➢ You are required to hold an active license to earn compensation (money, gift cards, free rent), even if it is from a family member.
- ○ Exemptions – when a real estate license is **not** needed:
  - ➢ Self-dealing (FSBO / FLBO) - individual or entity (owner, W-2 Employee or Officer)
  - ➢ Power of attorney or lawyer acting in the regular course of his/her practice
  - ➢ Appraisers, mortgage brokers, trustees, executors or administrators of an estate
  - ➢ Salaried employee of a property management broker, the mere crier of sale at an auction, or a housing authority.
- ○ It is important to ask "Is the person/entity earning compensation on behalf of another? If yes, then a license is required. If no, then a license is not required.

 A license is required to receive compensation for referrals. Compensation includes money as well as gifts that have value (use of a beach house for the weekend, concert tickets, swimming pool season pass, gift certificates, iPad, discounted rent, etc.).

- ○ Requirements to obtain Provisional License:
  - ➢ Must be at least 18 years old, a US citizen or non-citizen national or a qualified alien under federal law.
  - ➢ Pass a minimum 75 hour Prelicense course approved by the NCREC or provide evidence of experience in real estate that the Commission deems equivalent.

- ➢ Make application and pay fee, including a background check.
- ➢ Pass the NC Licensing Examination
- ➢ Pass the Character Review of the NCREC

- ○ Activities of Unlicensed Assistants
  - ➢ A licensed broker may hire an unlicensed assistant for day to day clerical activities, however, remains liable for their actions.
  - ➢ Property for Sale – an unlicensed assistant may perform clerical duties such as answering phones, data entry (as long as licensee filled out the form), filling flyer boxes, etc., however is **not permitted** to show listed property or hold an open house.
  - ➢ Property for Lease – an unlicensed assistant may perform clerical duties as noted above and is permitted to show property to potential tenants and fill out pre-printed lease forms, however **cannot negotiate** changes to the lease terms.

[1 QUESTION] – License Category and Status – BIC, Broker, Provisional Broker, Firm, Limited Non-resident Commercial Broker, Active / Inactive Status

License Categories:

- ➢ Provisional Broker – licensee that has not completed 90 hours of Postlicensing education. Must be affiliated with a supervising broker-in-charge to be active. When a provisional broker completes all 3 postlicensing classes provisional status will be removed automatically.
- ➢ Broker – a licensee that has completed 90 hours of Postlicensing Education.
- ➢ Broker-in-Charge (BIC) – broker, not on provisional status, responsible for supervising provisional brokers as well as brokerage compliance (all brokers) with agency disclosure and advertising laws.

  ⚠ **How many licenses? One broker license – multiple "status" types. All licensees are Brokers – depending on his/her status the broker will be Full, Provisional or Broker-In-Charge (BIC Eligible).**

- ➢ Firm License – any form of business <u>other than a Sole Proprietorship</u> must have a qualifying broker and a separate firm license. A Partnership, Limited Partnership (some partners have limited liability and limited power), S-Corp (limited liability, income flows to individual tax return), Corporations (limited liability, possibility of double taxation) and LLC's must have a Firm License. Each office location must have a Broker-in-Charge.

 A sole proprietorship does not require a separate firm license. All other entities – partnership, corporation, limited liability companies (LLC) – require a separate firm license and the appointment of a qualifying broker.

➢ Limited Non-Resident Commercial License – limited to commercial transactions (lease or purchase). The broker must be licensed in good standing and reside in another state, affiliate with a NC brokerage and send declaration to the Real Estate Commission. The broker cannot serve as a Broker-in-Charge and must deliver all trust money to their NC Broker-in-Charge.

 Many State Exam testing candidates are not familiar with the requirements for a Limited Non-Resident Commercial License.

o Active vs. Inactive
   ➢ Active – Current (paid $$), affiliated with a BIC (if provisional), met Postlicensing Education Requirements and Continuing Education Requirements.
   ➢ Inactive – Current (paid $$) <u>and</u>
       o Has decided not to affiliate with a BIC (if provisional), or
       o The Broker or Provisional Broker failed to complete CE by the June 10th deadline (which means that all activity must cease by June 30th) – must take current year and make up deficiency for the previous year – (max 16 hrs) if completed prior to 2 years, or
       o The Provisional Broker failed to complete Postlicensing Education – the licensee must make up the deficiency in order to activate.
       o **<u>Inactive licensees</u> are not required to take Postlicensing or Continuing Education until they are ready to activate their license, but must pay the $45 license renewal fee.**
       o When a license has been inactive for more than 2 years, the broker must complete 8 hours of continuing education and 60 hours of postlicensing classes before sending in request to activate.

[1 QUESTION] – Broker-in-Charge – Requirements, responsibilities and supervision of provisional brokers.

- o Broker-in-Charge (BIC) – a full Broker with at least 2 years full time experience or the equivalent over the past 5 years that has elected to become BIC. The experience can be gained while on provisional status. Must complete a 12 hour BIC course within 120 days of election or within the preceding year. The BIC is required to supervise all Provisional Brokers as well as ensure compliance with agency disclosure and advertising of all Brokers.

- o A non-provisional broker operating as a sole proprietorship is not required to become a BIC, however would not be able to list property for sale or rent, advertise services orally or in print, advertise referral services or manage rental property for others. A non-provisional broker cannot have a trust account for client money.

[1 QUESTION] – North Carolina Real Estate Commission – Purpose, composition and powers.

- o Purpose: To protect the general public in their dealings with real estate brokers. This is accomplished by:
  - ➤ Licensing real estate brokers and brokerage firms
  - ➤ Registration of time share projects
  - ➤ Approving schools to conduct Prelicensing, Postlicensing and Continuing Education programs approved by the Commission.
  - ➤ Providing information and education relating to the real estate business to licensees and the public.
  - ➤ Regulating the business activities of brokers and brokerage firms including disciplinary actions (Reprimand, Censure, Suspend and Revoke).

- o Composition of the Commission – 973211
  - ➤ 9 members, 7 appointed by the governor, 3 – (at least) active in real estate, 2 – (at least) not directly or indirectly involved in real estate, 1 appointed by the Speaker of the House, and 1 appointed by the President Pro-Tempore of the Senate. (973211)
  - ➤ Serve a 3-year term. Terms are staggered.
  - ➤ Chairman selected annually by members.
  - ➤ Receive a per diem but no salary for service.

- Powers: Reprimand, Censure, Suspend or Revoke Real Estate License.
  - Commission cannot fine <u>licensees</u> for violations of license law.
  - Commission can fine a <u>timeshare developer</u> for violation of the Time Share Act.
  - Commission can seek an injunction against an unlicensed party that is engaging in brokerage activity through legal action in superior court.

 Only the Real Estate Commission can act against your license – Reprimand, Censure, Suspend or Revoke (RCSR). A court can only recommend that a licensee lose his/her license. The Commission grants the license and the Commission can take it away. Licensee must respond to a complaint within 14 days.

 The Real Estate Commission does not currently have the ability to fine licensees (although they can fine time shares developers if they fail to register the time share project).

 The Real Estate Commission does not get involved with commission disputes between brokers. Those disputes are typically handled through the local REALTOR® Association.

- The Commission CANNOT:
  - Practice law
  - Declare contracts (sales, listing or leases) void
  - Regulate commission or how fees will be shared between licensees
  - Fine licensees for violations of License Law
  - Draft or prescribe real estate contract forms (they can only prescribe what needs to be in a form)
  - Act as a Board of Arbitration – to settle disputes between licensees or brokers and clients
  - Order a Broker to reimburse trust funds or compensate buyers or sellers for loss (only a court can)

[2 QUESTIONS] – License Administrative / Maintenance Requirements – Proof of license, change of name/address, reporting criminal convictions, license renewal/expiration/ reinstatement, continuing education and postlicensing education.

- o Selected Regulated Practices:
- ➢ Proof of License – All brokerages must display a copy of the firm license at all locations. All licensees are issued a pocket card that should be carried on his/her person at all times while engaged in real estate brokerage activity. A copy of the Firm's pocket card must be retained by the Qualifying Broker.
- ➢ Change of Name or Address – All licensees (both Brokers and Firms) must notify the Commission in writing of each change of name (personal or trade) or address, telephone number, or email address (personal or business) within <u>10 days</u>.
- ➢ Reporting Criminal Convictions – a licensee must report to the Commission within <u>60 days</u> of pleading guilty or being found guilty of a felony or misdemeanor. In addition, a licensee must report to the Commission any action taken by another professional license board (Appraisal Board, Bar Association, etc.).

- o Current vs. Expired - $$$
  - ➢ **All licenses automatically expire on June 30th unless the license is renewed within the preceding 45-day renewal period.**
  - ➢ Current – Paid license renewal fee by June 30th – no mailbox rule (must be received by the Real Estate Commission by June 30th). Online payment is required except in very limited circumstances.
  - ➢ Expired – Failed to pay license renewal fee – Expired is about $$$
    - Expired 6 months or less – pay 2 times the renewal fee (or $90) as the reinstatement fee and submit request to activate the license (affiliation with a brokerage or as an independent broker).
    - Expired for more than 6 months but less than 2 years – pay 2 times the renewal fee (or $90) as the reinstatement fee, submit a new application (including an updated background check), and one of the following: a) complete one postlicensing course within 6 months prior to submitting reinstatement application, b) pass both National and State licensing exams within 180 days of submitting reinstatement application or c) pass State only portion of the licensing exam if licensed in another state.

- Expired for more than 2 years – submit a new original application and full application fee $100 and pass both the National and State licensing exams. The licensee will be able to retain original license number and status at the time of expiration (full or provisional status) if completed within 3 years of expiration. When expired for more than 3 years, licensee will be on provisional status.

- ○ Education Requirements:
- ➤ Continuing Education Requirements - to remain on Active Status <u>must be completed by June 10th</u> of each license year (unless new licensed – first renewal is CE free). Provisional Brokers and Brokers that are not BIC - 4 Hour General Update + 4 Hour Elective. All BIC or BIC eligible brokers must take the Broker-In-Charge Update (BICUP) + 4 Hour Elective.
- ➤ Postlicensing Education Requirements (to remain on Active Status) – A provisional broker must successfully complete 1 of the 3 Postlicensing courses (Brokerage Relationships, Contracts and Closings, and Selected Topics) prior to their anniversary date (date of initial licensure). For example, if a provisional broker's license is issued on November 21, 2018 and they desire to remain on active status, at a minimum he/she must complete one of the courses prior to November 21, 2019 and then by the same period in 2020 and 2021. The courses may be completed sooner as long as they do not exceed more than 30-instructional hours in a 7-day period.
- ➤ A broker on inactive status that does not desire to become active is <u>not</u> required to take continuing or postlicensing education.
- ➤ A broker that fails to complete CE or Post by the required deadline will find it difficult to obtain an extension. Extensions are rarely granted and would not be approved due to a scheduling conflict.

 A new licensee desiring to maintain a license on active status will not be required to take CE classes until after his/her first license renewal. For example, a newly licensed provisional broker licensed on September 15, 2018 would renew his/her license by June 30, 2019 and would be required to complete CE by June 10, 2020 to maintain active status.

[3 QUESTIONS] – Agency Contracts and Practices – Requirements for Agency Contracts, Oral Buyer/Tenant Agency Contracts and Related Practices of Listing Agents and Agents Working with Buyers

Agreements That Must Be in Writing from Inception

o Listing Agreements

o Property Management Agreements

o Any agreement that seeks <u>EXCLUSIVITY</u> – limits the client from working with another broker.

 Written agreements must have a definite end date (listing agreement, buyer's agency agreement), however property management agreements may have automatic renewal.

 Must contain Non-Discriminatory (anti-discriminatory) language and the broker's license number.

Agreements That Can Be Oral at Inception

o Buyer Agency Agreements

o Tenant Representation Agreements

o Oral agency agreements do not have an end date.

o The buyer/tenant must orally agree to type of agency (exclusive, dual, designated) and the amount of compensation to be paid and by which party (buyer or seller).

 Must be reduced to writing _**no later than the time any party wants to extend an**_ _**offer**_ **to buy or rent.**

 Non-Exclusive...they can work with other brokers. Open Ended...no end date.

Common Forms of Agency Relationships

o <u>Exclusively Representing Seller</u> – where the firm represents only the Seller. Each agent within the office becomes a <u>Subagent</u> of the Seller and cannot represent a Buyer in the transaction.

   ➤ Agent owes all his/her loyalty and obedience to the Seller (as long as they comply with license and common law).

   ➤ Historically all agents worked for the Seller as they typically paid the listing agent and the agent that brought the buyer. This has significantly changed over the past few decades. The <u>payment of commission does not create agency</u> – that can only be accomplished by express agreement.

 If a Seller's Agent learns of personal or confidential information about the Buyer they have an <u>obligation</u> to disclose this information to the Seller (ie: that the buyer is willing to pay more). Additionally, the Seller's Agent <u>cannot</u> disclose information about the Seller (ie: that a Seller will take less than the asking price or that the Seller is currently delinquent on their mortgage), unless it rises to the level of a material fact (short sale or foreclosure notice has been sent).

 If a buyer <u>customer</u> seeks guidance about restrictive/protective covenants or whether an activity or action is permitted, you can provide them with a copy of the covenants. However, since you are the Exclusive Seller Agent, you cannot help them determine if the property will meet their needs. You will need to refer the third party/customer to an Attorney.

- o Exclusively Representing Buyer – where the firm represents only the Buyer and cannot represent the Seller in the transaction.
  - ➤ Agent owes all his/her loyalty and obedience to the Buyer (as long as they comply with license and common law).
  - ➤ This option is becoming more common in today's real estate market.

  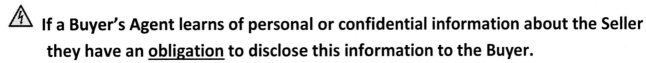 **If a Buyer's Agent learns of personal or confidential information about the Seller they have an <u>obligation</u> to disclose this information to the Buyer.**

- o Dual Agency – where the firm represents both the buyer and seller in the same transaction.
  - ➤ <u>Cannot advocate</u> for one party over the other. Cannot tell the buyer what to offer or the seller what to accept.
  - ➤ Cannot share personal or confidential information about the buyer to the seller or the seller to the buyer, unless it rises to the level of a material fact.

   A broker can share confidential information about the buyer and seller with other brokers of the firm. The confidential information cannot be shared between the buyer and seller. It is advisable not to share confidential information whenever possible in the event that a designated dual agency situation arises or is desired.

- o <u>Designated Dual Agency</u> – where the firm represents both the buyer and the seller in the same transaction, however the agent for the buyer and agent for the seller can advocate for his/her client's interest.
  - ➤ Cannot have personal or confidential information about the opposite party at the time of designation.
  - ➤ A provisional broker and his/her supervising broker-in-charge cannot act as designated agents (they can only be dual agents), as the BIC will become aware of personal information about the PB's client.

  This topic will be discussed further under Dual and Designated Agency.

[2 QUESTIONS] – Agency Disclosure – Providing Agency Brochure, First Substantial Contact, Disclosure of status by Seller's Agent and Buyer's Agent, Agency and Common Law, Disclosure Exceptions, Material Facts, Misrepresentation/Omission

Agency Disclosure

- o <u>Agent to Potential Client/Customer</u> - In a real estate transaction, whether residential or commercial, it is paramount for all parties to know how they will be working together. In fact, under North Carolina License Law a licensee is forbidden to provide brokerage services until agency has been determined. Agents are required to review the **Working with Real Estate Agents Brochure (WWREA)** at <u>First Substantial Contact</u> (FSC). FSC can occur in person, over the phone or electronically. It is the point in time that the discussion shifts from facts about the property to the buyer's needs or desires and financial ability to complete a purchase (personal and confidential information).

  - ➤ Seller's Agent to Seller – prior to discussing personal or confidential information. Often the first thing an agent should review prior to giving the listing presentation.
  - ➤ Open House – agent is not required to provide the WWREA brochure immediately when a prospective purchaser enters the home. Refer to the definition of FSC above.
  - ➤ Buyer's Agent to Buyer – prior to discussing personal or confidential information. Typically, a broker will meet a potential buyer in the office, provide the brochure and determine if they will act as a buyer's agent or subagent.
  - ➤ If disclosure is not made in person, a copy of the form must be transmitted within 3 <u>days</u> either by mail, fax or email.

- The WWREA brochure is <u>NOT</u> a contract. It explains agency and the different ways in which a broker can represent a client. It does not explain the typical process or transaction flow of buying or selling a home.
- The prospective client or customer is not obligated to sign the form unless they are acknowledging Seller Sub-agency representation (that the agent will work WITH them not FOR them).

 The WWREA is not required in ALL real estate transactions. Auctions and lease transactions are exempt.

- <u>Buyers Agent to Seller or Seller's Agent</u> – A buyer's agent must disclose their agency status to the seller or seller's agent upon <u>Initial Contact</u>. Initial Contact can occur at any time such as gathering information about the property, scheduling an appointment or may occur as late as the presentation of an offer.

 Students sometimes confuse First Substantial Contact (listing agent to buyer) and Initial Contact (buyer's agent to seller or seller's agent).

 First substantial contact is triggered by disclosing terms that could impact a party's bargaining position, like the need to relocate soon or facing financial difficulties.

Agency and Common Law
- Common Law – is the body of law that governs the relationship between the principal (client) and the agent (you).
  - Duties Owed to Principal – O.L.D. C.A.R. –Obedience, Loyalty, Diligence, Confidentiality, Accounting, Reasonable Skill, Care, And Diligence
    - Obedience – agent must follow the principal's lawful instructions.
    - Loyalty – agent must place the client's interest above all others.
    - Disclosure - agent must disclose material facts to all parties involved in the transaction. In addition they are required to present all offers, both written and oral.
    - Confidentiality - An agent cannot disclose personal or confidential information that would weaken their client's bargaining position (unless a material fact).
    - Accounting – agent must account for all money or property entrusted to them.

- Reasonable Skill, Care, Diligence – agent must be competent and knowledgeable about the type of real estate being sold, leased or exchanged and the area that the property is physically located.

➤ Duties Owed to 3rd Party Customers – H.F.D. – Honest, Fairness, Disclosure of Material Facts. This is where an agent works WITH a client, not FOR a client.
- The agent cannot prepare a market analysis as the recommend price would be the list price.
- The agent may provide unadjusted raw data about recently sold property from the multiple listing service.
- Should the buyer ask about the ability to make changes to the property (addition, storage shed, fence), the agent may provide a copy of the restrictive / protective covenants and refer the buyer to an attorney.

➤ Duties the Principal Owes the Firm – Good Faith (cooperation, truthfulness) and Compensation ($$). If a Principal Seller refuses to pay the commission that has been earned by the agent(s), the attorney or firm cannot withhold the funds from the Seller and should never advise the Buyer not to honor the purchase contract. Remember there are typically have 3 contracts in play –
- 1) Offer to Purchase and Contract between the Buyer and Seller
- 2) Listing Agreement between the Seller's Agent and Seller
- 3) Buyer Agency Agreement between the Buyer's Agent and Buyer.

If the Buyer were to breach the purchase contract with the Seller as a result of the Seller's refusal to pay commission, the Buyer would be liable for damages (loss of the earnest money with the seller retaining the due diligence fee). The closing attorney cannot force the Seller to pay the commission, however the Seller would be subject to a lawsuit to recover the commission, legal expenses and interest.

➤ Vicarious Liability - The Principal can be held liable for civil damages for the actions of his/her agent or subagent (tort) in the event the agent breaches duties to a third party.
- The brokerage (agency) agreement establishes the relationship and the scope of the agent's authority to act on behalf of the principal. All written agreements must define the firm's duties to the principal and provide for a definite end date.
- Agency agreements are between the Principal (Client) and the Firm.

The Principal is the party that contracts with the Firm to represent them (Seller – Listing Agreement, Buyer – Buyer Agency Agreement, Landlord – Property Management Agreement, or Tenant – Tenant Representation Agreement).

 There can be confusion about <u>Obedience</u>. We must follow our client's <u>lawful</u> instructions. Under License Law and Commission Rules, we must present all offers and a seller cannot relieve us of that responsibility. In addition, a seller cannot direct us to disclose a buyer's offer to another as we cannot do this without the express permission of the buyer who made the offer.

 The Listing Agreement/Buyer's Agency Agreement are owned by the FIRM. What happens if you leave? That would depend on your independent contractor agreement.

Other Terms:

- Material Fact – a fact that would affect the buyer's decision to buy or the seller's decision to sell. Some examples include a leaky roof, that zoning may change, roads may be widened, issues related to drainage or septic problems, or other condition issues related to the property.
  - The N.C. Real Estate Commission has determined that certain items are material facts that must be disclosed – meth labs, leaking polybutylene piping – even if repaired or replaced, and synthetic stucco (EIFS) – even if totally replaced. In addition, a seller must disclose if they have or plan to sever mineral rights prior to closing.
  - Some items in North Carolina are not a material fact – such as the presence of a sex offender in or near the property, that the property is stigmatized (death or violent crime), or that the house is haunted.
  - An agent cannot disclose if the current or previous occupants or owners had HIV or AIDS as this falls under State and Federal Fair Housing protected class (Handicap).

   A Seller's agent working WITH a buyer (not FOR) is required to disclose to the seller the fact that a buyer is willing to pay more than the amount stated in the offer. Working WITH a buyer (seller sub-agency) is very different from working FOR a buyer (as exclusive or dual agent – meaning an agency contract has been formed).

A Seller's agent working WITH a buyer will violate License Law and agency common law if they disclose to the buyer that seller will accept less than the listing price (without prior permission from the seller) or if the agent seeks to obtain the lowest possible price for the buyer, as the agent represents the seller and owes him/her loyalty.

o An agent is responsible to disclose things that they know or reasonably should have known. Failure to disclose or providing false information falls under the following categories:

➢ Willful – Agent acted with <u>intent</u> to purposefully lie or withhold information. The act of purposefully not seeking additional information about something that is a material fact would also fall under this category.

➢ Negligent – Agent made an unintentional error regarding material information or failed to disclose something that they reasonably should have known.

➢ Misrepresentation – Agent tells a lie. They have said something and it is wrong. **Opened Mouth.**

➢ Omission – The Agent fails to relate material information to the client/customer. **Did not Open Mouth.**

 A Seller tells the listing agent that there is a foundation issue but instructs the agent not to disclose. If the agent complies is he/she liable for this non-disclosure? (Hint: willful omission)

 Make sure to thoroughly review the examples included on pages 4-7 of the License Law and Commission Rule Comments, included at the end of this summary section.

o Puffing – making a statement that is exaggerated or that is objective and not easily verifiable. For example, an agent states in an ad that "This is the best house in the County". Some prospective buyers may agree and other may feel it is the best house to knock down. Puffing does not constitute misrepresentation.

- Dual Agency – Occurs when the <u>firm</u> that practices dual agency has an agency agreement with <u>both the Buyer and the Seller,</u> and they have expressly agreed to dual agency representation.

  - There is a slight reduction in the duties an agent is permitted to perform.
  - The Agent(s) must treat both parties fairly and equally by not advocating for one party over another – cannot discuss matters relating to price or terms of sale other than those offered.
  - Dual agents cannot pass personal or confidential information about one party to the other unless it rises to the level of a material fact. They can prepare a Comparative Market Analysis but cannot tell a Buyer what to offer nor a Seller what to accept.
  - If agreed to by the Seller at the time that they sign the Listing Agreement, then must be in writing.
  - If agreed to by the Buyer, then oral agreement is permitted while the Buyer Agency Agreement is oral, however it must be reduced to writing prior to the presentation of an offer.
  - A broker cannot act for more than one party in a transaction without the knowledge of all parties for who he or she acts (93A-6(a)(4)). Undisclosed Dual Agency is illegal.

  ⚡ **If dual agency is agreed to later (after initial refusal), then the determination of when it must be in writing is dictated by the Buyer's Agency Agreement. The Seller can orally agree to dual agency if, and only if, the Buyer Agency Agreement is oral. If the Buyer's Agency Agreement is in writing, then the seller authorization of dual agency must be in writing.**

  ⚡ **Dual agency cannot exist when the buyer and seller are represented by different firms.**

  ⚡ **It is important to understand when dual agency arises. When does a buyer's agent become a dual agent? A buyer represented by the firm is interested in purchasing a property listed with the same firm. When does a listing agent become a dual agent? A buyer represented by the same firm becomes in interested in purchasing his/her listing.**

- o <u>Designated Agency</u> – A form of dual agency – there cannot be designated agency without dual agency. The Principal must authorize both dual and designated agency. When permitted, the agents can return to their traditional advocacy roles similar to exclusive seller and exclusive buyer representation.
  - ➤ The designated agents are appointed by the Broker-in-Charge or firm policy and the agents cannot currently have personal or confidential information that would weaken the bargaining position of the other party.
  - ➤ Designated agency cannot be practiced by the Broker-in-Charge and a Provisional Broker under his/her supervision.
  - ➤ Brokers cannot designate if they are aware of personal / confidential information about the other party – they must remain dual agents.

[3 QUESTIONS] – Selected Regulated Practices – Advertising, Delivery of Instruments, Retention of Records, Drafting Legal Instruments, Disclosure of Offers and Broker Price Opinions

- ➤ Advertising Restrictions – No <u>blind ads</u>
  - o You must identify the brokerage you are affiliated with whether a sole proprietorship or entity.
  - o Brokers cannot advertise without the permission of his/her supervising BIC
  - o Brokers must get permission from the seller to display signs on the property, use a lockbox, and advertise on the internet.
  - o Providing only the licensees name, email address or website is not sufficient.
- ➤ Delivery of Instruments – All contracts (listing, buyer agency and offer to purchase) must be delivered within 3 days from the date of execution to the client/customer and BIC. The broker must provide a copy of the closing disclosure within the same timeframe unless provided by the attorney.
- ➤ Property Managers are relieved of the responsibility to provide copies of each lease when they provide a summary of the lease within 45 days and a copy of the lease within 5 days upon request, under the Standard NCAR Property Management Agreement.
- ➤ Retention of Records – 3 years from date of last activity (although recommended that you keep them longer and if you ask an attorney…forever). This includes the Working with Real Estate Agents brochure panel, listing agreements, buyer agency agreements, all versions of a contract (offer, counter-offer or offers), trust account records, and closing statements.

- ➤ Drafting Legal Instruments – licensees are not permitted to draft legal instruments. They must use a standard form prepared by an attorney or the Standard North Carolina Association of Realtors (NCAR if a REALTOR®) forms or refer the client to an attorney.

   A broker should NEVER draft provisions (lease or purchase) for a party for whom he or she is working for even if the provision is dictated by his/her client. A broker can have the client add the provision in the client's own handwriting so that the client cannot object about the provision later. It is always recommended that a broker recommend and refer the client to an attorney. The broker must refrain from giving advice regarding the language a party may want to add to a contract.

- ➤ Disclosure of Offers – A seller's agent is permitted, with the seller's permission, to disclose the <u>existence</u> of other offers and whether the other offers are from himself/herself or another broker within their firm. A broker **cannot disclose the price or any other material terms** of a buyer's offer without receiving consent of the buyer that made the offer.

   Material terms other than price include the closing date, that the offer is a cash deal, the amount of due diligence, etc.

- ➤ Broker Price Opinion – A provisional broker cannot complete a broker price opinion (BPO) or comparative market analysis (CMA) <u>for a separate fee</u>, in addition to commission earned from the sale or lease of the property. A broker that is not on provisional status may receive compensation for a BPO/CMA in addition to any commission earned from the sale or lease of the Property. The licensee must have direct access to sales data, it cannot be used for the purpose of originating a debt, limitations must be detailed on the work product (no access to the inside) and there cannot be a conflict of interest.

[1 QUESTION] – Handling & Accounting for Funds – Basic Trust Accounts

- o **Trust Funds**
- ➤ Real Estate Companies are not required to maintain a trust account unless they are engaged in a transaction that requires one (holding trust funds, property management, etc.).

- When a company elects to have a trust account, funds must be held in a bank that is federally insured and approved to do business in North Carolina (no longer required to have a physical location). The bank must make the records available to the Commission in event of an audit.
- A provisional broker must immediately deliver all trust money to his/her BIC.
- Other People's Money – earnest money, security deposits, monthly rent, repair funds
- Cannot <u>commingle</u> funds – mixing other people's money with your own - other than an amount to cover monthly fees and a little extra to cover fees for bounced checks (typically $100).
- Cash must be deposited immediately but no later than 3 banking days following receipt.
- EMD and Tenant Security Deposits (other than cash) must be deposited the later of 3 banking days following acceptance of the offer to purchase/lease or receipt (as you can't deposit what you don't have). The licensee must safeguard the EMD or Security Deposit until contract acceptance by delivering funds to his/her BIC.
- Rent, Settlement Proceeds and Other Trust Funds must be deposited within 3 banking days of receipt. NOTE: A broker may use the same trust account for general brokerage and property management, including managing several different properties with different owners (and that it does not constitute commingling – unless the broker is using the trust account for properties that are owned by him/her).
- A separate trust account is required for each Homeowner Association that is managed by a brokerage.
- Due diligence funds received by a broker for delivery to their client cannot be deposited into a brokerage trust account, but must be promptly delivered to the seller.

 It is important to know when cash and earnest money for a sales contract must be deposited in the trust account. Be careful to read test questions carefully as they may use calendar days, business days or banking days. Trust funds are to be deposited the later of 3 banking days from receipt or effective date of contract.

[1 QUESTION] – Brokerage Fees and Compensation – Disclosure of Compensation, Compensation of Unlicensed Persons for Brokerage Activities, and Commission's Limited Role Regarding Broker Compensation

➢ Compensation paid to a brokerage is outlined in the buyer's agency agreement or listing agreement. Commission splits are based upon the independent contract agreement that a licensee has with his/her firm.

➢ Compensation (commission, referral fee, etc.) cannot be paid to an individual or entity that does not hold an active real estate license at the time compensation is earned, except for a fee paid to a travel agent for vacation rental reservations. Recall that compensation is earned when the property goes under contract or the seller receives an offer that meets all his/her desires, not when the sale closes.

➢ Disclosure of Additional Compensation – A broker must disclose to his/her principal/client any payment (cash, check, gift card, iPad, dinner vouchers, etc.) from 3rd parties that are in addition to compensation outlined in the agency agreement. Disclosure must be made in a timely fashion (may be oral)– with sufficient time to aid a reasonable person's decision-making. The disclosure should be reduced to writing no later than the Offer to Purchase and includes both monetary and non-monetary compensation (trips, gift certificates, etc.).

➢ The NC Real Estate Commission will not hear complaints regarding commission disputes between licensees. The licensees, if REALTORs, must file a grievance with the local board of REALTORs.

[3 QUESTIONS] – Prohibited Practices

o The Commission can take action against a licensee that violates license law. In addition, they can seek injunctive relief if an unlicensed individual is performing an activity that by law would require a license.

o Grounds for Disciplinary Action (Suspension or Revocation of License):
  ➢ Obtaining a license under false pretenses.
  ➢ Licensee is convicted of felony, including failure to report the conviction within 60 days
  ➢ Violating license law or if an unlicensed employee violates license law
  ➢ Making willful/negligent misrepresentations or omissions of material facts
  ➢ Making false promises
  ➢ A Provisional Broker accepting compensation from anyone other than his/her BIC

- A Broker representing more than one party in a transaction without consent
- Failing to account for all funds belonging to others
- Being untrustworthy or incompetent so as to endanger the general public
- Paying compensation (monetary or otherwise) to an unlicensed person
- Fraudulent, improper or dishonest dealing
- Performing legal services for clients, e.g. no drafting of contracts
- Commingling personal funds with trust funds
- Failing to deliver documents timely (immediately but no later than 5 days) or retaining documents for the prescribed time (3 years from the date of last activity)
- Violating any rule or regulation published and distributed by the Commission
- Giving a check to the Commission that is returned unpaid (insufficient funds)

 The Commission can commence proceedings to suspend or revoke a broker's license when payment for license renewal is dishonored by the bank.

[1 QUESTION] – Time Shares – Definition, Registration, Criminal Penalty, Project Broker, Public Offering Statement, Purchaser's Right to Cancel, Commission's Authority & Disciplinary Action, Registrar, Records, Agency Agreements and Disclosure, Handling / Accounting for Funds.

- o **Time Shares**
- 5 / 5 / 5 / 10 – 5 non-consecutive periods, over 5 or more years, where the buyer has 5 days to terminate the contract and the developer must retain the purchase money in the escrow (trust account) for 10 days.
- Nonconsecutive means a break in the days that you stay. Timeshares are often referred to as interval ownership, meaning not continuous. Some timeshares allow the owner to stay every-other year. To be deemed a timeshare the owner must have the use for 10 or more years.
- Projects must be registered with the NCREC – failure to do so while offering or selling timeshares is a <u>felony</u> offense.
- A <u>project broker</u> supervises licensed brokers that sell time share properties with duties that are like a broker-in-charge.
- An active real estate license is required to earn compensation selling time shares, on behalf of another. There is not a separate time share license.

- Each time share developer must disclose in a public offering statement – the total financial obligation of the purchaser including the purchase price and other charges, who can raise fees and for what reason, the date of availability of uncompleted facilities, the term of the timeshare, right to terminate within 5 days of execution, etc.
- Violations of license law by a timeshare developer results in a fine of $500 per occurrence

 Deposits and other fees paid by a buyer must be held in the escrow account for 10 days. The buyer has 5 days to terminate the contract.

 There is not a separate Time Share License.

Other North Carolina Laws and Practices – 11 Questions

[2 QUESTIONS] – Property Taxation – Legal Requirements, Excise Tax (no calculation)

- o **Property Taxation**
- The <u>Machinery Act</u> provides for real property taxation based upon the assessed value but does NOT set the rate of taxation (which is based on the municipalities tax base and budget requirements).
- Special Assessment – may be public or private. Commonly charged for the installation of water and sewer lines, paving, sidewalks, street lights, etc. for the public or replacement or maintenance of common area items if private through the HOA. Schools are <u>not</u> funded by special assessments, rather the city or county will issue bonds.

- o **Excise Tax**
- Tax assessed by the State on the sale of real property that is paid by the Seller. In North Carolina, the tax is $1 per $500 of the sales price.

 NC Counties and municipalities may adjust both the assessed value and the property tax rate every year. The assessed value of a property is based upon the fair market value of the property at the time of the assessment. It MAY be adjusted every year, however MUST be adjusted every 8 years (octennial reappraisal).

[2 QUESTIONS] – Sales Contracts and Practices – Basic Concepts and Provisions of the NCAR/NCBA Offer to Purchase and NC Practices Related to Sales Contracts

Sales Contracts and Practices

- Brokers will most often utilize the Standard NCAR / NCBA Offer to Purchase and Contract (OPC) for residential sales (single family, 1-4 unit dwelling, condo or townhouse) or use a form prepared by an attorney. **BROKERS CANNOT DRAFT contracts or provisions to a contract. Brokers are not required to use the NCAR/NCBA OPC.**
- Major Provisions of the Standard NCAR/NCBA OPC
  - ➢ Sales Price and Method of Payment
  - ➢ Adequate Property Description
  - ➢ Provision for Fixtures that do not convey and will be retained by Seller and Personal Property that will be transferred to the Buyer
  - ➢ Due Diligence – the period of time that a buyer has to investigate a property (inspection, survey, appraisal), apply for financing, and negotiate repairs. This period of time is referred to as the Due Diligence Period (DDP). During this period the Buyer may terminate the contract for any reason or no reason at all. The DDP is "time is of the essence" meaning a drop dead date – if the buyer does not terminate by 5:00 p.m. on that date, the earnest money deposit will no longer be refundable. The contract is heavily in favor of the buyer until the due diligence period expires and then becomes heavily in favor of the seller.
  - ➢ Due Diligence Fee – an agreed upon amount, _if any_, for the right to perform due diligence and allow the buyer the right to terminate the contract during the DDP. It is not required to form a legally binding contract, is not refundable (unless the Seller breaches), and is credited to the Buyer at closing. There is no guidance as to the amount. The property and overall market conditions will dictate if a fee is paid and the amount. The DDF is made payable directly to the Seller and becomes the Sellers on the "effective date" of contract.
  - ➢ Earnest Money Deposit (EMD) – although not required to form a legally binding contract, it is money deposited with an escrow agent to demonstrate that the buyer will act in good faith. It may be paid when the contract is initially formed, within 5 days of execution, or it can be paid later (additional EMD). The contract details how EMD will be treated:

- Credited to buyer upon closing
- Refunded to the buyer upon termination of contract prior to the expiration of the Due Diligence Period – Buyer must provide written notice by 5:00 P.M on the Due Diligence Period date.
- Earnest money will serve as <u>liquidated damages</u> (defined in the contract) that the Seller will receive in the event of breach of contract by buyer (the Seller's sole and exclusive remedy for breach – EMD and retention of DDF).
- Must be refunded if the Seller breaches the contract – refuses to sell, property is damaged, a condition of the contract is not met.

 Failure to deliver the EMD or DDF, or if either payment is returned for insufficient funds by the bank, <u>does not</u> automatically terminate a contract. The Seller must make written demand and the Buyer then has 1 Banking Day to provide good funds.

 What happens if the buyer signs a promissory note for the EMD? Is this part of the Mortgage? (Hint: It is possible and will only be secured financing if that is specifically detailed in an exam question. A promissory note is just an IOU and not a form of secured financing.)

➢ The Seller is to provide a <u>GENERAL WARRANTY DEED</u> and legal access to a public right of way.

➢ Settlement/Closing Date – Settlement is when paperwork is signed (Settlement = Sign). Closing is when the title record is updated, recorded and the bank provides a funding number to release funds (when the transaction includes a residential loan according to the Good Funds Settlement Act (Closing = Cash).

    Settlement Date is <u>NOT</u> "time is of the essence". Either party may delay for <u>14 days</u> as long as they are making best efforts.

➢ Repairs – note that the Seller is not obligated to agree to make repairs. If the Seller agrees to repairs it must be in writing and signed by both parties. It becomes a part of the contract and should the seller fail to perform they will be deemed to have breached the contract. It is paramount that the Buyer complete all the Due Diligence and Repair Negotiations during the DDP to avoid the loss of the EMD.

- Signatures and Dates – 1 to buy, 2 (or more) to sell. The contract must be signed by both the buyer and seller and the date of acceptance should be clearly shown. It is important to remember to initial and date all changes to prove the date that the contract was formed (effective date). To have a valid contract all Sellers must sign and agree to the sale.

- Other Important Topics:
  - A broker must submit all offers immediately (but no later than 3 days) from receipt and has no authority to reject an offer (even if the Seller has instructed the broker to reject offers below a certain price – as this would be a violation of NC License Law and Commission Rules).
  - The broker cannot disclose the price or other material terms of a buyer's offer to another buyer without the express permission of the buyer that made the offer.
  - If a broker receives multiple offers he/she should never instruct the Seller to counter all of them at the same time as this could potentially create multiple contracts and legal disputes should more than one party accept. A broker must present all offers and then the Seller can decide to accept, reject or counter one of the offers, or could request that buyers bring their "highest and best" offer. Agents have a duty to treat all buyers equally.
  - If a property is already under contract, a buyer may submit an offer and include the Back-Up Contract Addendum. The Back-Up Contract only becomes binding when the primary contract fails. The Seller cannot accept the Back-Up and then terminate the primary contract without being in breach. The Buyer may withdraw the contract at any time prior to receiving notice that the primary contract failed and he/she is moving up in position.
  - A broker can NEVER reference commission (compensation) or disclaim liability in an Offer to Purchase and Contract.
  - Counteroffer (may become binding when acceptance is communicated) vs. Memo-to-Buyer (not binding unless the Seller accepts the new offer)
  - A legally binding contract is formed when there is a written offer, written acceptance and communication over the wall of separation to the offering party (call, email, text). It is common to see multiple questions regarding contract formation based on certain scenarios (has a legally binding contract been formed or when was a legally binding contract formed).

The Mail Box Rule states that the postmark date is the effective date of a contract so long as it is addressed to the other party or their agent (seller responds to the buyer or buyer's agent), unless contract states acceptance must be received by a certain date.

1 QUESTION] – Closing Procedures – Attorney Supervised Closings, Typical Pre-Closing and Closing Procedures, NC Good Funds Settlement Act and the Broker's Responsibility as to Settlement Statements

Closing the Real Estate Transaction

- Prior to closing a buyer will want to complete inspections, surveys and other investigations to determine if the property will meet his/her needs. This should be completed during the due diligence period, providing enough time for negotiations. The seller is not required to negotiate for repairs.

   For testing purposes, it is important to remember that one reason a lender typically requires a survey is to determine if the property is in a flood zone or if there are any encroachments to the property.

- Settlement Method – is the most common method in NC where the Attorney, the buyer and buyer's agent, and the seller and seller's agent meet to transfer the property. Note that physical attendance by all parties is not required as long as all documents have been signed and funds delivered.

- The NCREC would consider a broker who fails to attend the settlement meeting with his/her client to have violated their fiduciary duties to that client.

- An Agent should review the settlement statement with his/her buyer or seller client to ensure that the Buyer knows the amount of certified funds to bring to closing and to determine if the seller agrees with amount of proceeds or certified check they may need to bring to closing. <u>The best source for verifying the accuracy of the closing disclosure is the sales contract.</u>

 It is important to note that the Agent is not responsible for verifying <u>EVERY</u> amount on the closing statement, however is generally responsible for verifying the statements accuracy. The agent is responsible for what they know or reasonably should have known.

- Funds and keys do not change hands until <u>closing</u> – the attorney performs a title search, title is updated, recorded and the lender releases funds to the attorney in accordance with the **Good Funds Settlement Act**.

[2 QUESTIONS] – Laws Governing Residential Tenancies – NC Residential Rental Agreement Act, Laws Governing Eviction Procedures, NC Tenant Security Deposit Act and Statute of Frauds (as to Leases)

- North Carolina Residential Rental Agreement Act – The landlord must provide <u>safe, fit and habitable premises</u> to a tenant that is renting a residential dwelling. This includes complying with building codes, maintenance and repair of appliances, electrical, plumbing and HVAC systems among others.
    - Landlord must provide working smoke detectors and one carbon monoxide detector per rental unit that has an attached garage or fossil fuel burning appliance/fireplace (and replace batteries at the beginning of the tenancy). New rules require the landlord to use 10-year lithium batteries or hardwire detectors with battery backup.
    - The Tenants must keep the premises clean and remove their trash, maintain the plumbing fixtures but not repair, if leaking and not damage the property (except for normal wear and tear). Tenants must replace the batteries in the smoke and carbon monoxide detector during the tenancy.

- No Retaliatory Eviction – the landlord cannot seek eviction of a tenant for exerting his/her right to safe, fit and habitable premises by requesting repairs. This protection lasts up to 12 months.
- Eviction proceedings are typically held in small claims court and heard by a <u>Magistrate</u>.
- Types of Eviction:
    - Summary Ejectment – where the landlord seeks <u>actual eviction</u> of the tenant for breach of lease (often for the failure to pay rent). The owner can sue for failure to pay however all action will stop if the tenant pays the back rent amount plus late/court fees. The owner can also sue for the breach of the agreement, where the tenant may still be evicted even if he/she pays the back rent and other fees. The landlord must use JUDICIAL means and cannot "Self Help" by turning off utilities, changing the locks, or seizing or placing the tenant's belongings on the curb.
    - Constructive Eviction – when the owner fails to maintain safe, fit and habitable premises. This remedy is not available when the tenant has damaged the property

(they would be responsible for the repairs). For example, if the HVAC system fails and the owner has not taken steps to correct the matter, even though the tenant provided written notice. The tenant can elect to move out without penalty and sue the landlord for the cost of the move, temporary housing, and recovery of rent paid while the unit was not habitable. The tenant can elect to stay (however has to still pay) and can seek action through the court or by reporting the violation to the Housing Department. The tenant cannot make the repair and then bill the landlord.

- o North Carolina Tenant Security Deposit Act – law that limits the amount that can be charged which is determined by the length of the lease agreement, the types of charges that are allowable against the deposit (not for normal wear and tear), and where the security deposit must be held (trust or escrow account or bonded).
  - ➤ The maximum security deposit is 2 weeks for week to week, 1.5 months for month to month, and 2 months for anything greater.
  - ➤ Reasonable pet deposits are allowed, however cannot be charged for service dogs or therapeutic animals.
  - ➤ The landlord or property manager can charge back rent, late fees, damages to the premises (above normal wear and tear), period of time the unit is not rented during the lease rental period, court costs/legal fees, and the costs of re-renting the premises against the security deposit. **The funds cannot be used until the lease has terminated and access is regained**.
  - ➤ A detailed accounting of the charges must be provided within 30 days of the termination of the tenancy. If the final costs have not been tallied, an interim accounting must be provided in 30 days and a final accounting must be provided within 60 days of termination.
  - ➤ The security deposit must be held in a trust or escrow account if handled by a licensee. A non-licensee may elect to be bonded. If the security deposit is not handled in this manner the landlord/property manager loses the right to charge <u>any</u> of the cost outlined above against the security deposit.
  - ⚠️ **Leases that exceed 3 years must be in writing under the Statute of Frauds and must be recorded to be protected against 3rd parties under the Connor Act.**

[1 QUESTION] – Residential Square Footage Guidelines – No Calculations

Residential Square Footage Guidelines

- Square Footage – the North Carolina Real Estate Commission (NCREC) does not require an agent to disclose the square footage of a building, however many MLS's do require this information. If an agent discloses the square footage it must be accurate. The listing agent is primarily responsible however a buyer's agent may be held responsible if a reasonable agent could identify the error (agents are responsible for what they know or reasonably should have known).

  - ➤ Square Footage is reported as <u>Living Area</u> and Other Area and commonly broken down for above and below grade. Under the NCREC **Residential Square Footage Guidelines** agents should <u>use outside measurements</u> whenever possible. When not possible, agents may take interior measurements then add 6 inches to any outside wall.

  - ➤ Unpermitted square footage should be reported to the buyer as this is a material fact (safety concerns and potential expense to bring work up to code).

  - ➤ <u>H</u>appy <u>F</u>eet <u>D</u>ance <u>A</u>lways – How to remember the definition of <u>Living Area</u> – <u>H</u>eated, <u>F</u>inished, and <u>D</u>irectly <u>A</u>ccessible. Additionally, the ceiling height must be 7ft (6ft 4in under ducts or beams) and if the ceiling is sloped – 50% or more must be 7 ft. or greater and if so can include to where the ceiling height is 5 ft.

  - ➤ Townhouse – take inside measurements then add 6 inches for any exterior or party wall.

  - ➤ Condo – only take inside measurements. A condo owner owns the airspace only. Do not add 6 inches.

   Note HEATED square footage is included...it is not a requirement that a property be air conditioned.

[3 QUESTIONS] – Miscellaneous Laws and Concepts

- Tenancy by the Entirety - Can only exist between a husband and a wife. The surviving spouse automatically has the right of survivorship without passing through probate. A will cannot defeat the right of survivorship. Divorce terminates Tenancy by the Entirety and the former husband and wife will own as Tenants-in-Common. Separation does not impact tenancy by the entirety ownership. This type of tenancy is the only one that does not have the right of partition.

⚠️ **If a married couple purchases property in NC and fail to specify the type of ownership, they will own as Tenancy by the Entirety.**

o Townhouses - ownership of the individual unit as well as the land that it rests upon including the party walls. The common areas are owned by the Homeowner's Association.

o Residential Property and Owner's Association Disclosure – as the name implies is for residential sales (1-4 units), whether the property is listed with a broker or offered for sale by the owner. <u>The seller completes the form NOT the agent</u>. The broker has a duty to disclose material facts. They would never use the disclosure form to meet this obligation as this form is for the seller.

➢ The Seller can select Yes, No or No Representation for each question on the form which addresses specific questions about the property and seeks disclosure of problems or defects.

➢ The Seller can lawfully select No Representation for each item on the disclosure form even if the seller has actual knowledge of defects pertaining to the property.

➢ The Seller is not obligated to disclose anything (except for Lead Based Paint, EIFS, Meth, Polybutylene piping when leaking and severance of oil/mineral/gas rights during their ownership). NC is a <u>Caveat Emptor</u> state meaning "let the Buyer beware"; this includes items that may be considered material facts.

➢ There are exemptions for new construction, foreclosure, transfers among family and transactions where the buyer is already occupying the residential dwelling.

⚠️ **The responsibility falls upon the agent to disclose what they know or reasonably should have known about the property.**

⚠️ **Even if a Seller selects "No Representation" it does not relieve the agent of the responsibility to "Discover and Disclose" material facts.**

⚠️ **If a Seller fails to deliver the form or provides it after contract, the buyer will have a rescission period – the earliest of 3 calendar days from the date of receipt, 3 calendar days from the date of contact, or possession/closing.**

o Mineral and Oil and Gas Rights Mandatory Disclosure – the Seller must inform the buyer if they have severed rights or intend to sever rights prior to closing on the property. In addition, the seller can select yes, no, or no representation relating to previous owners severance of rights.

- Subdivision Regulations - <u>Subdivision Regulations</u> – The definition of a subdivision is a tract of land divided into two or more lots for resale or development. Subdivisions must be approved by city planning department and city council as it can increase the costs of a municipality (for schools, trash removal, police protection, etc.). Prior to offering lots for sale you must determine if the plat has <u>Preliminary Approval</u> before accepting a contract or earnest money. Lots cannot close until <u>Final Approval</u> has been obtained and recorded. The sale of lots in an unapproved subdivision can result in criminal penalties.
- The subdivision developer must disclose if streets will be public or private.
- <u>Road Maintenance Agreement</u> – NC law requires the disclosure of the party that is required to maintain the roads, which must be made in writing. A developer must state whether roads will be public or private. The mere fact that roads are built to NCDOT standards does not guarantee that the roads will be "Public" roads (maintained by tax dollars). Roads must be built to NCDOT standards, dedicated to NCDOT and then must be accepted by NCDOT. Note: An offer of dedication does not automatically ensure acceptance by DOT or municipality.
- <u>Restrictive / Protective Covenants</u> - a private land use restriction placed on a property (also called <u>Deed Restrictions</u>) often placed in deeds by the developer to create conformity in a neighborhood. Restrictions are commonly for minimum square footage, architectural designs, approved color schemes, etc. They are enforced by the homeowners' association (HOA) or by an owner within the neighborhood. Compliance is typically sought by the HOA by giving notice or seeking compliance through court action (injunction – to stop the offense). There is no need to prove direct harm.
  - Covenants pass with the land upon transfer, so they are binding upon future owners.
  - The existence of covenants is a material fact that must be disclosed.
  - Can be terminated by 100% agreement of property owners in the subdivision (or some lesser amount outlined in the covenants).
  - The right to enforce can be lost through <u>Laches</u> where the HOA or homeowners failed to enforce in a timely manner.

  ⚡ **Restrictive/protective covenants are often more restrictive than zoning or planning. The sheriff's department, department of housing, planning and zoning do <u>NOT</u> hear complaints about non-compliance.**

  ⚡ **The homeowner or HOA sues for an INJUNCTION to stop the party that is violating the restrictions.**

- On-Site Septic Systems – a broker should verify with the Health Department the approval for the septic system and the number of bedrooms that the lot <u>Perked</u> for. The number of bedrooms advertised is limited to the soil suitability test result and type of system installed. There are many types of systems (conventional, sand filter, spray, etc.) and they involve varied levels of ongoing costs and maintenance and therefore should be disclosed as a material fact.

General Real Estate Topics (5 Questions)

[2 QUESTIONS] – Basic House Construction – Wood-Frame Construction Methods & Terminology and Architectural Styles

Architectural Styles

- There are many types of architectural styles in residential real estate. Some of the most common types are: one story or ranch style, split level, 1.5 story or cape cod, 2-story homes (colonial, French provincial, etc.). There is not any style that is superior to another as buyer preference is key to determining style needs.
- Single-story homes cost more per square foot to build than other types of construction.

Residential Construction

- Building Codes – minimum construction standards for new construction, renovations or additions. It is very important to follow permitting requirements. This is an area of significant focus in practice and is the "new mold".
- General Contractors License – required of an individual or entity when building a structure costing more than $30,000.
- Properties that have an air handler and ductwork have a forced air HVAC system.

Basic Terminology:

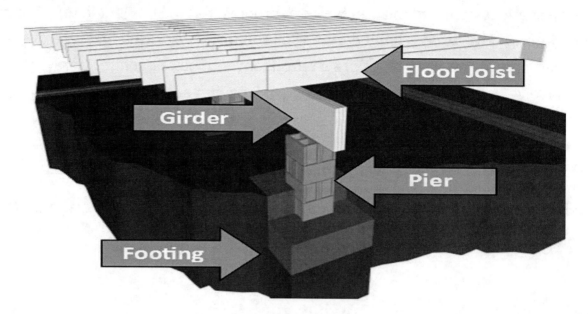

- ➢ Footing – A concrete support that forms the base of the foundation that is poured below the frost line under the surface of the ground and used to distribute weight evenly. Hint: What is the base of your foundation? Your **foot**'ing!!
- ➢ Piers – a foundation column that supports the floor framing over an open span between the foundation walls.
- ➢ Girder – Heavy wooden member or steel beam that typically runs across the top of the piers and supports the floor joists. Hint: Think Girdle – holds up the center…and a girder holds up the center.
- ➢ Joists – part of the floor framing - attached to the sill.

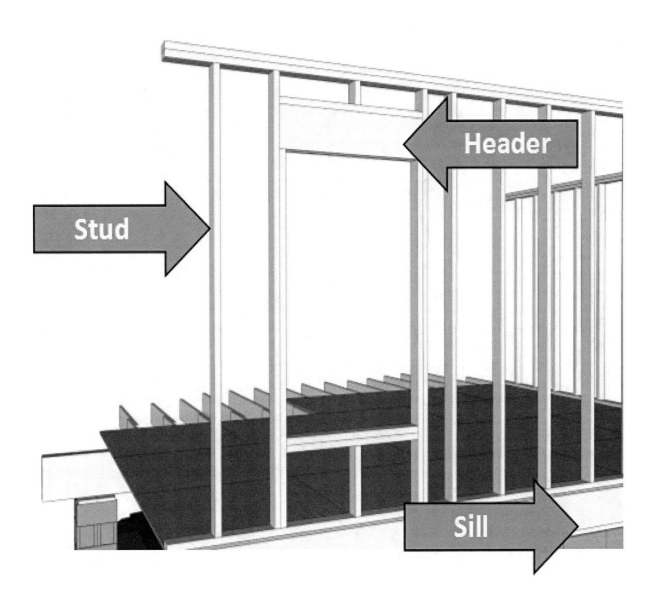

Test questions can ask about a specific item or test construction omponents of the wall or foundation, etc.

Wall Components:

➤ Studs – Part of the wall framing, commonly 2" x 4" wood that is attached to the sill plate.

➤ Header – Support beam located above openings – typically doors and windows – meant to strengthen the wall by spreading the weight.

➤ Sill or Sill Plate – lowest wooden member in home construction that rests upon the foundation wall and on top of the piers.

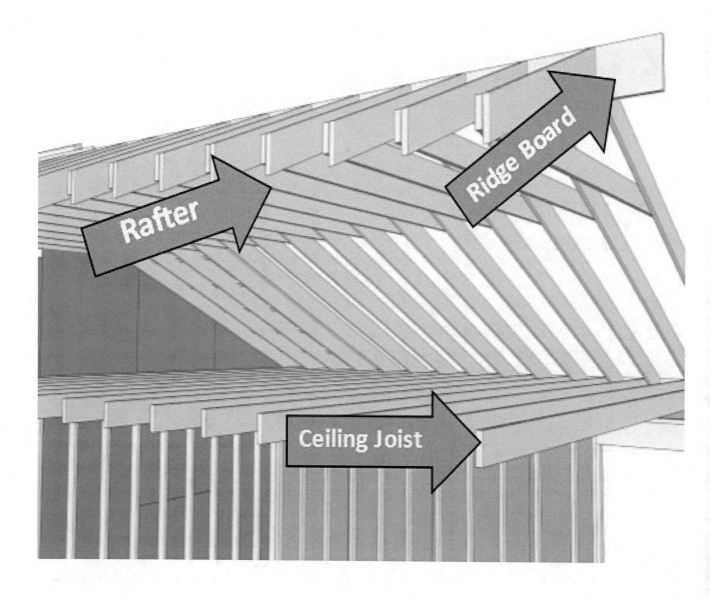

- ○ Roof Components:

  - ➤ Sheathing – the wooden layer attached to the roof rafters (and wall studs); most often plywood or OSB.
  - ➤ Roof Pitch – the slope of a roof is calculated as the rise over run.
  - ➤ Ridge Board – often tested as the highest wooden member in roof construction that is fastened to the ends of the rafters.
  - ➤ Rafter – a type of beam that supports the roof that extends from the ridge to the wall plate.
  - ➤ Flashing – sheet metal that protects the building from water damage – found around chimneys.

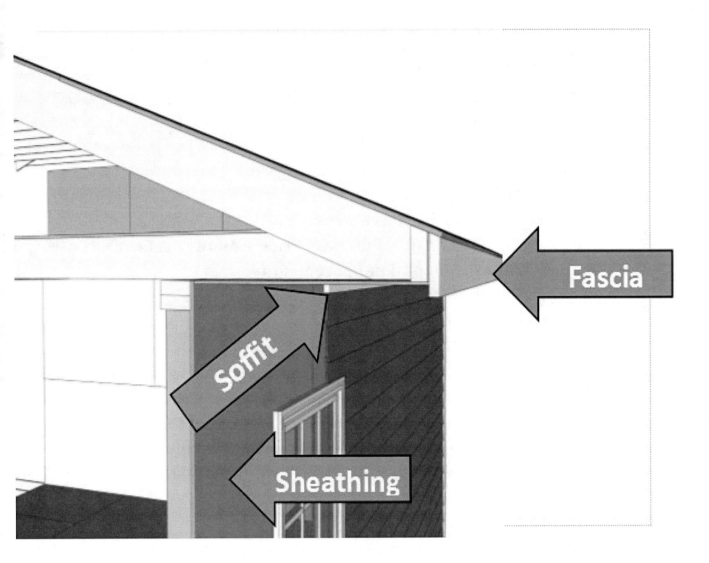

- o Eave – the overhang of the roof over the wall stud.
  - ➤ Fascia – component of the eave that faces out and where the gutter is typically attached to.
  - ➤ Soffit – the flat board attached to the eave.

Other Terms:
- o Windows – contain muntins – horizontal bars separating glass panes, mullions – vertical bars separating glass panes and sashes – framed part of window that holds glass in place.
- o Septic System – require percolation test (**perc or perk**) to determine the suitability of the soil and which system will work, if any, to ensure proper leaching takes place. Soil suitability permits are issued by the local health department and detail a specific number of bedrooms the dwelling can have.

[1 QUESTION] – Federal Taxation of Home Ownership/Sale

- o You are commonly tested on what expenses may be deducted on the current years' federal income tax return and what the gain is for a particular property. (no calculation – however need to know terminology)
  - ➢ Tax Deduction = Property Taxes, Interest and Points. (When points are paid at closing they can be deducted in the calendar year, on refinance points are deducted over the life of the loan.)
  - ➢ Calculation of gain is done in three steps:
    1. **Calculate Adjusted Basis = Purchase Price + Allowable Closing Costs (not finance charges) + Capital Improvements**
    2. **Calculate Amount Realized = Sales Price – Commission – Allowable Closing Costs (not repairs)**
    3. **Calculate Gain = Amount Realized – Adjusted Basis.**
    Note: Notice that discount points and mortgages do not factor into capital gain calculation.
- o Taxation on the gain from the sale of a principal residence receives special tax treatment – as long as it is your primary residence for 2 out of the last 5 years, you can exclude $250,000 of gain if single / $500,000 of gain if married. This exemption cannot be used more than once every 2 years. Gains in excess of the exclusion will be taxed at long-term capital gain rates.
- o Capital Gains Rates – 12 months or less – short term gain taxed at ordinary rates / More than 12 months – capped at 15%

[1 QUESTION] – Residential Loan Qualification Calculations – Qualifying a Buyer Using Given Income/Expense Ratios

Qualifying Calculation:

The Rules:

- You must convert the income/expenses to the same time (take annual income and divide by 12 so that you have monthly income).
- This way you are comparing monthly expenses to monthly income.
- When a conventional loan is obtained by the buyer, the typical qualifying ratios are 28% Housing and 36% Total Debt.
- Monthly Income X 28% = Maximum Housing Payment (PITI + HOA Dues)
- Monthly Income X 36% = Maximum Total Debt Payment (Housing + Long Term Debt)
- The buyer qualifies when the payment is equal to or less than the maximum amount.
- The borrower must qualify under both ratios to qualify for the loan.

[1 QUESTION] – Comparative Market Analysis Calculations

CMA Calculations:

The Rules:

- Do Not adjust the subject property
- If the Comp has Positive (Superior) features ***subtract***
- If the Comp has Negative (Inferior) features ***increase***
- You may be required to adjust the comp for appreciation
- Note: You may place more weight on the value of homes that are very similar to the Subject property.
- You may be asked to calculate a range of value – the principles remain the same for adjustments.

Calculation of Appreciation:

- First calculate appreciation for year:
  Sold Price X Appreciation Rate
- Then calculate monthly:
  Appreciation for Year/12
- Appreciation Entry:
  Monthly Appreciation X # of Months

Cost Approach to Value:

The Rules:
- o Do not depreciate land. This is typically added at the end after calculating the value of the property adjusted for depreciation.

Calculation:
- o <u>Cost of Building New</u>:
  Square Footage X Cost Per Square Foot
- o <u>Then calculate Remaining Life Percentage</u>:
  [(Economic Life – Effective Age) / Economic Life]
- o <u>Adjusted Value</u>:
  [Building New X Remaining Life Percentage] + Land Value + Improvements

Valuing Property Using Income Capitalization Method:

Calculating NOI is a G.I.V.E.N.:
- o Gross Income – Vacancy – Expenses = Net Operating Income
- o Note that Gross Income – Vacancy = Effective Gross Income (**which is often used as a distractor**)
- o Expenses = Operating Expenses which do not include capital improvements, depreciation, or debt service

Calculation of Value:
- o Value = NOI / Cap Rate

Gross Rent Multiplier:

The Rule:
- o Gross Rent Multiplier = Sales Price / Monthly Gross Income

Calculation:
- o <u>Value</u>:
  Monthly Gross Income X Gross Rent Multiplier

Gross Income Multiplier:

The Rule:

- o Gross Income Multiplier = Sales Price / Yearly Gross Income

Calculation:

- o <u>Value:</u>

  Yearly Gross Income X Gross Income Multiplier

ACKNOWLEDGEMENTS

Thank you to Chris Barnette and Kandyce Ellis for their contributions and review of the workbook. Your insight helped us create a better resource for students and for that we say thank you.

Matt Davies is a North Carolina real estate instructor and began teaching in 2008. He is an active real estate broker and obtained his broker license in 2003. Matt teaches prelicense, postlicense and continuing education courses using multiple approaches to help students understand difficult topics. Matt has a Bachelor of Science in Business Administration with a concentration in Accounting from Bryant University. Prior to entering real estate, Matt worked for PricewaterhouseCoopers, LLP.

Tiffany Stiles has been educating students of all ages for many years, and has recently become an instructor for real estate prelicense, postlicense and continuing education courses. Tiffany obtained a Bachelor of Science in Industrial Engineering from Florida State University, with a minor in Mathematics and continued to get her Masters of Science in Industrial & Systems Engineering from Georgia Institute of Technology, before getting her real estate license in 2001. Tiffany is committed to improving student's success and confidence by simplifying difficult topics.

LICENSE LAW AND RULES COMMENTS

Comments on Selected Provisions of the
North Carolina Real Estate License Law
and Real Estate Commission Rules

INTRODUCTION

These comments on selected North Carolina Real Estate License Law and Real Estate Commission Rules provisions are intended to assist real estate licensees, prelicensing course students and others in understanding the License Law and Commission rules. The comments are organized in a topic format that often differs from the sequence in which the topics are addressed in the License Law and Commission rules. The topics selected for comment here are not only of particular importance in real estate brokerage practice but also are likely to be tested on the real estate license examination. The appropriate references to the License Law and Commission rules are provided beside each listed topic.

REQUIREMENT FOR A LICENSE
General [G.S. 93A-1 and 93A-2]

Any person or business entity who directly or indirectly engages in the business of a real estate broker for compensation or the promise thereof while physically in the state of North Carolina must have a North Carolina real estate broker license. In North Carolina, a real estate licensee may only engage in brokerage as an "agent" for a party to a transaction. Thus, a real estate licensee is commonly and appropriately referred to as a real estate "agent" even though the latter term does not actually appear in the License Law. Note that a real estate "licensee" is NOT automatically a "REALTOR®." A licensed real estate agent is a REALTOR® **only** if he/she belongs to the National Association of REALTORS®, a private trade association. Thus, the term REALTOR® should not be used to generally refer to all real estate licensees.

License Categories [G.S. 93A-2]

There is only one "type" of license, a **broker** license; however, there are several license status categories as described below:

Provisional Broker – This is the "entry level" license status category. A person who has met all the license qualification requirements (including a *75-hour prelicensing course and passing the Commission's license examination*) is initially issued **a broker license on "provisional" status** and is referred to as a **"provisional broker."** A provisional broker generally may perform the same acts as a broker whose license is NOT on provisional status so long as he or she is supervised by a broker who is a designated **broker-in-charge**. A provisional broker may not operate independently in any way. G.S. 93A-2(a2) defines a **"provisional broker"** as "...*a real estate broker who, pending acquisition and*

documentation to the Commission of the education or experience prescribed by G.S. 93A-4(a1), must be supervised by a broker-in-charge when performing any act for which a real estate license is required."

This license status category is comparable to a "salesperson" license in most other states except that it is a **temporary license status category**. Provisional brokers may not retain this status indefinitely – they must complete required **postlicensing education** (one 30-hour course each year for the three years following initial licensure – total of 90 hours) to remove the "provisional" status of their licenses and to remain eligible for "active" license status.

Broker – A "provisional broker" who satisfies all postlicensing education requirements to terminate the "provisional" status of such license becomes a **"broker"** without having to take another license examination. A broker is NOT required to be supervised by a broker-in-charge in order to hold an "active" license. An applicant who is a licensed broker in another US jurisdiction may be licensed directly as a North Carolina **broker NOT on provisional status** by passing the "State" section of the North Carolina license examination. All others must first be licensed in North Carolina as a **provisional broker** and then satisfy the postlicensing education requirement to become a non-provisional broker.

Most frequently, brokers elect to work for another broker or brokerage firm. Brokers may also elect to operate independently as a sole proprietor; however, with limited exceptions, such broker will have to qualify for and designate himself or herself as a **broker-in-charge** in order to operate independently and perform most brokerage activities (discussed further below under "broker-in-charge" and also in a subsequent section on brokers-in-charge that appears near the end of this appendix).

Broker-In-Charge – G.S. 93A-2(a1) defines a **"broker-in-charge"** as "...*a real estate broker who has been designated as the broker having responsibility for the supervision of real estate provisional brokers engaged in real estate brokerage at a particular real estate office and for other administrative and supervisory duties as the Commission shall prescribe by rule.*" Commission Rule A.0110 requires that each real estate office must have a broker who meets the qualification requirements to serve as "broker-in-charge" of the office and who has designated himself or herself as the broker-in-charge of that office. As is the case with "provisional broker," "*broker-in-charge" is not a separate license, but only a separate license status category*. A broker who is to serve as the broker-in-charge (BIC) of an office (including working independently) must be designated as a BIC with the Commission.

North Carolina Real Estate License Law and Commission Rules

To qualify for designation as a broker-in-charge, a broker's license must be on "active" status but NOT on "provisional" status, the broker must have **two years full-time or four years part-time brokerage experience within the previous five years** (or education/experience the Commission finds equivalent to such experience), and the broker must complete a 12-hour **Broker-In-Charge Course** no earlier than one year prior or 120 days after designation. Broker-in-charge requirements are addressed in detail in a separate subsequent section titled "Broker-In-Charge."

Limited Nonresident Commercial Broker – A broker or salesperson residing in a state other than North Carolina who holds an active broker or salesperson license in the state where his or her primary place of real estate business is located may apply for and obtain a North Carolina **"limited nonresident commercial broker license"** that entitles such licensee to engage in transactions for compensation involving "commercial real estate" in North Carolina. While the non-resident limited broker will remain affiliated with his/her out of state real estate company and will not have a North Carolina broker-in-charge, the non-resident licensee must enter into a "notification of broker affiliation" and a "brokerage cooperation agreement" with a resident North Carolina broker not on provisional status and the licensee must be supervised by the North Carolina broker while performing commercial real estate brokerage in North Carolina. Like a "firm" license, a limited nonresident commercial broker license is a separate license.

Licensing of Business Entities [G.S. 93A-1 and 2; Rule A.0502]

In addition to individuals (persons), "business entities" also must be licensed in order to engage in real estate brokerage. Any corporation, partnership, limited liability company, association or other business entity (other than a sole proprietorship) must obtain a separate real estate **firm** broker license.

Activities Requiring a License [G.S. 93A-2]

Persons and business entities who for consideration or the promise thereof perform the activities listed below as an agent for others are considered to be performing brokerage activities and must have a real estate license unless specifically exempted by the statute (see subsequent section on "Exemptions"). There is no exemption for engaging in a limited number of transactions. A person or entity who performs a brokerage service in even one transaction must be licensed. Similarly, no fee or other consideration is so small as to exempt one from the application of the licensing statute when acting for another in a real estate transaction. *Brokerage activities include*:

1. **Listing (or offering to list) real estate for sale or rent**, including any act performed by a real estate licensee in connection with obtaining and servicing a listing agreement. Examples of such acts include, but are not limited to, soliciting listings, providing information to the property owner, and preparing listing agreements or property management agreements.

2. **Selling or buying (or offering to sell or buy) real estate**, including any act performed by a real estate licensee in connection with assisting others in selling or buying real estate. Examples of such acts include, but are not limited to, advertising listed property for sale, "showing" listed property to prospective buyers, providing information about listed property to prospective buyers (other than basic property facts that might commonly appear in an advertisement in a newspaper, real estate publication or internet website), negotiating a sale or purchase of real estate, and assisting with the completion of contract offers and counteroffers using preprinted forms and communication of offers and acceptances.

3. **Leasing or renting (or offering to lease or rent) real estate**, including any act performed by real estate licensees in connection with assisting others in leasing or renting real estate. Examples of such acts include, but are not limited to, advertising listed property for rent, "showing" listed rental property to prospective tenants, providing information about listed rental property to prospective tenants (other than basic property facts that might commonly appear in an advertisement in a newspaper, real estate publication or internet website), negotiating lease terms, and assisting with the completion of lease offers and counteroffers using preprinted forms and communication of offers and acceptances.

4. **Conducting (or offering to conduct) a real estate auction**. (Mere criers of sale are excluded.) NOTE: An auctioneer's license is also required to auction real estate.

5. **Selling, buying, leasing, assigning or exchanging any interest in real estate, including a leasehold interest, in connection with the sale or purchase of a business.**

6. **Referring a party to a real estate licensee, if done for compensation**. Any arrangement or agreement between a licensee and an unlicensed person that calls for the licensee to compensate the unlicensed person in any way for finding, introducing or referring a party to the licensee has been determined by North Carolina's courts to be prohibited under the License Law. Therefore, *no licensee may pay a finder's fee, referral fee, "bird dog" fee or similar compensation to an unlicensed person.*

Unlicensed Employees — Permitted Activities

The use of unlicensed assistants and other unlicensed office personnel in the real estate industry is very widespread and the Commission is frequently asked by licensees what acts unlicensed persons may lawfully perform. As guidance to licensees, the Commission has prepared the following list of acts that an unlicensed assistant or employee may lawfully perform so long as the assistant or employee is salaried or hourly paid and is not paid on a per-transaction basis.

North Carolina Real Estate License Law and Commission Rules

An unlicensed, salaried employee MAY:

1. Receive and forward phone calls and electronic messages to licensees.
2. Submit listings and changes to a multiple listing service, but only if the listing data or changes are compiled and provided by a licensee.
3. Secure copies of public records from public repositories (i.e., register of deeds office, county tax office, etc.).
4. Place "for sale" or "for rent" signs and lock boxes on property at the direction of a licensee.
5. Order and supervise routine and minor repairs to listed property at the direction of a licensee.
6. Act as a courier to deliver or pick up documents.
7. Provide to prospects basic factual information on listed property that might commonly appear in advertisements in a newspaper, real estate publication or internet website.
8. Schedule appointments for showing property listed for sale or rent.
9. Communicate with licensees, property owners, prospects, inspectors, etc. to coordinate or confirm appointments.
10. Show rental properties managed by the employee's employing broker to prospective tenants and complete and execute preprinted form leases for the rental of such properties.
11. Type offers, contracts and leases from drafts of preprinted forms completed by a licensee.
12. Record and deposit earnest money deposits, tenant security deposits and other trust monies, and otherwise maintain records of trust account receipts and disbursements, under the close supervision of the office broker-in-charge, who is legally responsible for handling trust funds and maintaining trust accounts.
13. Assist a licensee in assembling documents for closing.
14. Compute commission checks for licensees affiliated with a broker or firm and act as bookkeeper for the firm's bank operating accounts.

Exemptions [G.S. 93A-2(c)]

The following persons and organizations are specifically exempted from the requirement for real estate licensure:

1. A **business entity** selling or leasing real estate owned by the business entity when the acts performed are in the regular course of or are incident to the management of that real estate and the investment therein. This exemption extends to officers and employees of an exempt corporation, the general partners of an exempt partnership, and the managers of an exempt limited liability company when engaging in acts or services for which the corporation, partnership or limited liability company would be exempt.
2. A person acting as an **attorney-in-fact** under a power of attorney from the owner authorizing the final consummation of performance of any contract for the sale, lease or exchange of real estate. (Note: This limited exemption applies only to the final completion of a transaction already commenced. The licensing requirement may not be circumvented by obtaining a power of attorney.)
3. An **attorney-at-law** who is an active member of the North Carolina State Bar only when performing an act or service that constitutes the practice of law under Chapter 84 of the General Statutes. Thus, the attorney exemption is strictly limited and attorneys generally may NOT engage in real estate brokerage practice without a real estate license.
4. A person acting as a receiver, trustee in bankruptcy, guardian, administrator or executor or any person acting under a court order.
5. A **trustee** acting under a written trust agreement, deed of trust or will or the trustee's regular salaried employees.
6. **Certain salaried employees of broker-property managers.** (See G.S. 93A-2(c)(6) for details.)
7. An individual owner selling or leasing the owner's own property.
8. A **housing authority** organized under Chapter 157 of the General Statutes and any regular salaried employee with regard to the sale or lease of property owned by the housing authority or to the subletting of property which the housing authority holds as tenant.

THE REAL ESTATE COMMISSION

Composition [G.S. 93A-3(a)]

The Real Estate Commission consists of nine (9) members who serve three-year terms. Seven members are appointed by the Governor and two are appointed by the General Assembly upon the recommendations of the Speaker of the House of Representatives and the President Pro Tempore of the Senate. At least three (3) members must be licensed brokers. At least two (2) members must be "public members" who are NOT involved directly or indirectly in the real estate brokerage or appraisal businesses.

Purpose and Powers [G.S. 93A-3(a), (c) and (f); G.S. 93A-6(a) and (b);G.S. 93A-4(d) and 93A-4.1 & 4.2]

The principal purpose of the Real Estate Commission is to protect the interests of members of the general public in their dealings with real estate brokers. This is accomplished through the exercise of the following statutory powers granted to the Commission:

1. Licensing real estate brokers and brokerage firms, and registering time share projects.
2. Establishing and administering prelicensing education programs for prospective licensees and postlicensing and continuing education programs for licensees.
3. Providing education and information relating to the

real estate brokerage business for licensees and the general public.

4. Regulating the business activities of brokers and brokerage firms, including disciplining licensees who violate the License Law or Commission rules.

It should be noted that the Commission is specifically prohibited, however, from regulating commissions, salaries or fees charged by real estate licensees and from arbitrating disputes between parties regarding matters of contract such as the rate and/or division of commissions or similar matters. [See G.S. 93A-3(c) and Rule A.0109.]

Disciplinary Authority [G.S. 93A-6(a)-(c)]

The Real Estate Commission is authorized to take a variety of disciplinary actions against licensees who the Commission finds guilty of violating the License Law or Commission rules while acting as real estate licensees. These are: **reprimand, censure, license suspension** and **license revocation**. The License Law also permits a licensee under certain circumstances to surrender his/her license with the consent of the Commission. Disciplinary actions taken against licensees are regularly reported in the Commission's periodic newsletter which is distributed to all licensees and also may be reported in local and regional newspapers.

It should be noted that licensees may be subject to the same disciplinary action for committing acts prohibited by the License Law when selling, leasing, or buying real estate for themselves, as well as for committing such acts in transactions handled as agents for others. [G.S. 93A-6(b)(3)]

The Commission also has the power to seek in its own name **injunctive relief** in superior court to prevent any person (licensees and others) from violating the License Law or Commission rules. A typical example of when the Commission might pursue injunctive relief in the courts is where a person engages in real estate activity without a license or during a period when the person's license is suspended, revoked or expired. [G.S. 93A-6(c)]

Any violation of the License Law or Commission rules is a criminal offense (misdemeanor) and may be prosecuted in a court of law. However, a finding by the Commission that a licensee has violated the License Law or Commission rules does not constitute a criminal conviction. [G.S. 93A-8]

PROHIBITED ACTS BY LICENSEES

G.S. 93A-6 provides a list of prohibited acts which may result in disciplinary action against licensees. Discussed below are various prohibited acts, except for those related to handling and accounting for trust funds, broker's responsibility for closing statements, and the failure to deliver certain instruments to parties in a transaction, which are discussed in the subsequent sections on "General Brokerage Provisions" and "Handling Trust Funds."

Important Note

The provisions of the License Law relating to misrepresentation or omission of a material fact, conflict of interest, licensee competence, handling of trust funds, and im-

proper, fraudulent or dishonest dealing generally apply independently of other statutory law or case law such as the law of agency. Nevertheless, other laws may affect the application of a License Law provision. For example, the N.C. Tenant Security Deposit Act requires an accounting to a tenant for a residential security deposit within 30-60 days after termination of a tenancy. License Law provisions (and Commission rules) require licensees to account for such funds within a reasonable time. Thus, in this instance, a violation of the Tenant Security Deposit Act's provisions would also be considered a violation of the License Law.

Similarly, the law of agency and the law of contracts as derived from the common law may impact the application of License Law. Thus, a licensee's agency status and role in a transaction might affect the licensee's duties under the license law. Examples of how an agent's duties under the License Law may be affected by the application of other laws are included at various points in this section on "Prohibited Acts by Licensees."

Misrepresentation or Omission [G.S. 93A-6(a)(1)]

Misrepresentation or omission of a material fact by a licensee is prohibited, and this prohibition includes both "willful" and "negligent" acts. A "willful" act is one that is done intentionally and deliberately, while a "negligent" act is one that is done unintentionally. A **"misrepresentation"** is communicating false information, while an **"omission"** is failing to provide or disclose information where there is a duty to provide or disclose such information.

Material Facts

For purposes of applying G.S. 93A-6(a)(1), whether a fact is "material" depends on the facts and circumstances of a particular transaction and the application of statutory and/or case law. The Commission has historically interpreted **"material facts"** under the Real Estate License Law to include at least:

Facts about the property itself (such as a structural defect or defective mechanical systems);

Facts relating directly to the property (such as a pending zoning change or planned highway construction in the immediate vicinity); and

Facts relating directly to the ability of the agent's principal to complete the transaction (such as a pending foreclosure sale).

Regardless of which party in a transaction a real estate agent represents, the facts described above must be disclosed to both the agent's principal and to third parties the agent deals with on the principal's behalf. In addition, an agent has a duty to disclose to his or her principal any information that may affect the principal's rights and interests or influence the principal's decision in the transaction.

Death or Serious Illness of Previous Property Occupant — Note, however, that G.S. 39-50 and 42-14.2 specifically provide that the fact that a property was occupied by a person who died or had a serious illness while oc-

North Carolina Real Estate License Law and Commission Rules

cupying the property is NOT a material fact. Thus, agents do not need to voluntarily disclose such a fact. If a prospective buyer or tenant specifically asks about such a matter, the agent may either decline to answer or respond honestly. If, however, a prospective buyer or tenant inquires as to whether a previous owner or occupant had AIDS, the agent is prohibited by fair housing laws from answering such an inquiry because persons with AIDS are considered to be "handicapped" under such laws and disclosure of the information may have the effect of discriminating against the property owner based on the handicapping condition.

Convicted Sex Offender Occupying, Having Occupied or Residing Near a Property — Note also that the same North Carolina statutes (G.S. §39-50 and §42-14.2) that state the death or serious illness of a previous occupant of a property is not a material fact in a real estate transaction contain a similar provision relating to **convicted sex offenders**. The statutes provide that when offering a property for sale, rent or lease, "…it shall not be a material fact…that a person convicted of any crime for which registration is required by Article 27A of Chapter 14 of the General Statutes [statutes establishing registration programs for sex offenders and sexually violent predators] occupies, occupied or resides near the property; provided, however, that no seller [or landlord or lessor] may knowingly make a false statement regarding such fact." Therefore, an agent involved in a transaction is **not** required to volunteer to a prospective buyer or tenant any information about registered sex offenders as described above. If a buyer or tenant specifically asks about sex offenders in a neighborhood, an agent need only answer truthfully to the best of his/her knowledge. In the absence of a specific inquiry about this matter from the buyer, an agent representing the buyer who knows, for example, that a registered sex offender lives in the immediate area, will probably want to disclose the information in the interest of serving his/her buyer-client even though not required by law to do so. On the other hand, in the absence of a specific inquiry by the buyer, if the agent who knows such information represents the seller, the agent will probably want to check with his/her seller-client before disclosing that information since voluntary disclosure is likely not in the seller's best interest. Any agent also has the option of advising a prospective buyer or tenant about how to check the statewide sex offender registry online at www.sexoffender.ncdoj.gov/search.aspx.

This introductory information should assist in understanding G.S. 93A-6(a)(1), which establishes four separate (although closely related) categories of conduct which are prohibited. These are discussed below, and a few examples of prohibited conduct are provided for each category.

Willful Misrepresentation — *This occurs when a licensee who has "actual knowledge" of a material fact deliberately misinforms a buyer, seller, tenant or landlord concerning such fact.* A misrepresentation is also considered to be "willful" when a li-

censee who does NOT have actual knowledge of a matter material to the transaction provides incorrect information concerning such matter to a buyer, seller, tenant or landlord *without regard for the actual truth of the matter* (i.e., when a licensee intentionally provides information without knowing whether it is true and the information provided is in fact not true).

Note: The following examples of willful misrepresentation apply regardless of the licensee's status (seller's agent or buyer's agent) or role (listing agent or selling agent).

> **Example:** An agent knows that a listed house has a severe problem with water intrusion in the crawl space during heavy rains. In response to a question from a prospective buyer who is being shown the house during dry weather, the agent states that there is no water drainage problem.

> **Example:** An agent knows that the heat pump at a listed house does not function properly, but tells a prospective buyer that all mechanical systems and appliances are in good condition.

> **Example:** An agent knows that the approximate market value of a house is $225,000, but tells the property owner that the house is worth $250,000 in order to obtain a listing.

> **Example:** An agent is completely unfamiliar with the features or condition of a listed property; however, the agent informs a prospective buyer that the plumbing is in good working order without first checking with the owner. (The agent in such instance is acting without regard for the truth of the matter being represented. If the plumbing in fact needs significant repair, then the agent may be guilty of willful misrepresentation.)

> **Example:** Without checking with the owner, an agent tells a prospective buyer of a listed house that heating and cooling costs are "very reasonable." (Because the agent acted without regard for the truth of the matter, he may be guilty of willful misrepresentation if heating and cooling costs are in fact extraordinarily high.)

Negligent Misrepresentation — *This occurs when a licensee unintentionally misinforms a buyer, seller, tenant or landlord concerning a material fact either because the licensee does not have actual knowledge of the fact, because the licensee has incorrect information, or because of a mistake by the licensee. If a reasonably prudent licensee "should reasonably have known" the truth of the matter that was misrepresented, then the licensee may be guilty of "negligent misrepresentation" even though the licensee was acting in good faith.*

Negligent misrepresentation by real estate licensees occurs frequently in real estate transactions. A very common situation is the recording of incorrect information about a property in an MLS listing due to the negligence of the listing agent. When a prospective buyer is subsequently provided the incorrect information from the MLS by the agent working with the buyer, a negligent misrepresentation by the listing agent occurs.

North Carolina Real Estate License Law and Commission Rules

A listing agent is generally held to a higher standard with regard to negligent misrepresentation of material facts about a listed property to a buyer than is a selling agent who is acting as a seller's subagent. This is because (1) The listing agent is in the best position to ascertain facts about the property, (2) the listing agent is expected to take reasonable steps to assure that property data included with the listing is correct and (3) it is generally considered reasonable for a selling agent to rely on the accuracy of the listing data except in those situations where it should be obvious to a reasonably prudent agent that the listing information is incorrect. However, *a buyer's agent may in some cases be held to a higher standard than a seller's subagent because of the buyer's agent's duties to the buyer under the law of agency and the buyer's agent's special knowledge of the buyer's particular situation and needs.*

Example: An agent has previously sold several lots in a subdivision under development and all those lots passed a soil suitability test for an on-site septic system. The agent then sells Lot 35 without checking as to whether this lot satisfies the soil test; however, the agent informs the buyer that Lot 35 will support an on-site septic system when in fact the contrary is true. (While the agent's conduct may not rise to the level of willful disregard for the truth of the matter, the agent was at least negligent in not checking the soil test result on Lot 35 and is therefore guilty of negligent misrepresentation. This result is not affected by the agent's agency status or role in the transaction.)

Example: An owner tells a listing agent with ABC Realty that his house has 1850 heated square feet. Without verifying the square footage, the agent records 1850 square feet on the listing form and in the listing information published in the local MLS. The house is subsequently sold by a sales agent with XYZ Realty who tells the buyer that according to the MLS data, the house has 1850 square feet. The buyer later discovers that the house actually has only 1750 square feet. (In this situation, the listing agent did not make a direct misrepresentation to the buyer; however, he/she initiated the chain of communication which led to the buyer being misinformed, and thus indirectly misrepresented a material fact. Further, the listing agent's failure to verify the square footage constituted negligence. Therefore, the listing agent is guilty of a negligent misrepresentation. Although the selling agent directly communicated the incorrect information to the buyer, he/she probably acted reasonably in relying on the data in MLS. In this case, if the selling agent had no reason to doubt the MLS data, the selling agent is not guilty of a negligent misrepresentation. Note, however, that if the square footage discrepancy had been sufficiently large that a reasonably prudent selling agent should have known the listed data was incorrect, then the

selling agent would also have been guilty of negligent misrepresentation. The result in this particular example is not affected by the selling agent's agency status (seller's subagent or buyer's agent), although this might be a factor in other situations.

Willful Omission — *This occurs when a licensee has "actual knowledge" of a material fact and a duty to disclose such fact to a buyer, seller, tenant, or landlord, but deliberately fails to disclose such fact.*

Example: An agent knows that a zoning change is pending that would adversely affect the value of a listed property, but fails to disclose such information to a prospective buyer. The agent has committed a willful omission regardless of the agent's agency status or role in the transaction.
[**Note:** Information about a zoning change, planned major highway or similar matter that would significantly enhance the value of a seller's property must also be disclosed to the seller, even if the licensee is a buyer's agent.]

Example: An agent knows that the city has just decided to extend water and sewer lines to a subdivision that has been plagued for years by serious water quality and sewage disposal problems. This will result in a substantial increase in the value of homes in the subdivision. The agent, who is working with a buyer to purchase a house in the subdivision, does not inform the seller of the city's recent decision. The agent has committed a willful omission and this result is not affected by the agent's agency status or role in the transaction.

Example: An agent knows that a listed house has a major defect (e.g., crumbling foundation, no insulation, malfunctioning septic tank, leaking roof, termite infestation, or some other problem) but fails to disclose such information to a prospective buyer. The agent has committed a willful omission and this result is not affected by the agent's agency status or role in the transaction.

Example: A selling agent working with a buyer as a subagent of the seller learns that the buyer is willing to pay more than the price in the buyer's offer, but fails to disclose this information to the seller (or listing agent) when presenting the offer. The selling agent has committed a willful omission. If, however, the selling agent were acting as a buyer's agent, then the result would be different because the agent does not represent the seller and has a duty not to disclose to the seller confidential buyer information that would be harmful to the buyer's interest.

Example: A buyer's agent becomes aware that the seller with whom his buyer is negotiating is under pressure to sell quickly and may accept much less than the listing price. Believing such information should always be kept confidential, the buyer's agent does not provide

North Carolina Real Estate License Law and Commission Rules

the buyer with this information. The buyer's agent is guilty of a willful omission. An agent must disclose to his/her principal any information that might affect the principal's decision in the transaction.

Example: Suppose in the immediately preceding example that the seller's property is listed with the firm of the buyer's agent and the firm's policy is to practice traditional dual agency in in-house sales situations where it represents both the seller and the buyer. In this situation, the buyer's agent would not be considered to have committed a willful omission under the License Law by not disclosing the information about the seller's personal situation to the buyer. NOTE: This assumes, however, that the buyer's agent properly disclosed his/her status as a buyer's agent to the seller or seller's agent upon "initial contact," that dual agency was properly authorized by both the seller and buyer prior to showing the seller's property to the buyer, the authorization was timely reduced to writing in the agency agreements that also limit the disclosure of information in dual agency situations (as is the case with the agency agreement forms provided by the North Carolina Association of REALTORS® for use by its members).

Negligent Omission — *This occurs when a licensee does NOT have actual knowledge of a material fact and consequently does not disclose the fact, but a reasonably prudent licensee "should reasonably have known" of such fact.* In this case, the licensee may be guilty of "negligent omission" if he/she fails to disclose this fact to a buyer, seller, tenant or landlord, even though the licensee acted in good faith in the transaction.

The prohibition against negligent omission creates a *"duty to discover and disclose" material facts* which a reasonably prudent licensee would typically have discovered in the course of the transaction. *A listing agent is typically in a much better position than a selling agent to discover material facts relating to a listed property and thus, will be held to a higher standard than will a selling agent acting as a seller's subagent. On the other hand, a buyer's agent in some circumstances may be held to a higher standard than a seller's subagent because of the buyer's agent's duties to the buyer under the law of agency, particularly if the buyer's agent is aware of a buyer's special needs with regard to a property.* Again we see how the agency relationships between agents and principals to a transaction and the licensee's role in the transaction can affect a licensee's duties and responsibilities under the License Law.

Instances of negligent omission occur much less frequently than instances of negligent misrepresentation. This is because most facts about a listed property are recorded on a detailed property data sheet from which information is taken for inclusion in MLS listings. If incorrect information taken from an MLS listing is passed on to a prospective purchaser, then a "misrepresentation," rather than an "omission," has occurred. Nevertheless, there are examples of negligent omission which can be cited.

Example: A listing agent lists for sale a house located adjacent to a street that is about to be widened into a major thoroughfare. The thoroughfare project has been very controversial and highly publicized. The city recently finalized its decision to proceed with the project and the plans for the street widening are recorded in the city planner's office. A buyer, working with a selling agent, makes an offer to buy the house. The listing agent does not disclose the street widening plans to the buyer or selling agent and claims later that he/she was not aware of the plans. In this situation, both the listing and selling agents are probably guilty of negligent omission because each "should reasonably have known" of the street widening plans, clearly a material fact, and should have disclosed this fact to the buyer. This result is not affected by whether the selling agent is a buyer agent or seller's subagent.

Example: A seller has a 30,000 square foot commercial property for sale which cannot be expanded under local zoning laws. The buyer is looking for property in the 25,000 - 30,000 square foot range, but has told his buyer's agent that he needs a property where he can expand to 50,000 square feet or more in the future. The seller does not think to advise the buyer's agent that the property cannot be expanded, and the buyer's agent makes no inquiry about it although he is aware of the buyer's special needs. If the buyer purchases the property without knowing about the restriction on expansion, the buyer's agent is guilty of a negligent omission for failing to discover and disclose a special circumstance that the agent knew was especially important to his/her client.

Example: When listing a house, a listing agent is told by the seller that one area of the roof leaks badly when it rains, but the moisture so far is being contained in the attic. The listing agent forgets to note this on the MLS data sheet and forgets to disclose the leaking roof problem to prospective buyers and selling agents. The listing agent is guilty of a negligent omission. Because the agent's failure to disclose the leaking roof problem was unintentional, the listing agent is not guilty of a willful omission; however, his/her forgetfulness resulting in his/her failure to disclose the defect constitutes a negligent omission.

Making False Promises [G.S. 93A-6(a)(2)]

Real estate brokers are prohibited from "making any false promises of a character likely to influence, persuade or induce." The promise may relate to any matter which might influence, persuade or induce a person to perform some act he/she might not otherwise perform.

Example: An agent promises a prospective apartment tenant that the apartment will be repainted before the tenant moves in. The agent then fails to have the work done after the lease is signed.

Example: An agent promises a property owner that

North Carolina Real Estate License Law and Commission Rules

if he/she lists his/her house for sale with the agent's firm, then the firm will steam-clean all the carpets and wash all the windows. The firm then fails to have the work done after the listing contract is signed.

Other Misrepresentations [G.S. 93A-6(a)(3)]

Real estate brokers are prohibited from pursuing a course of misrepresentation (or making of false promises) through other agents or salespersons or through advertising or other means.

> **Example:** In marketing subdivision lots for a developer, a broker regularly advertises that the lots for sale are suitable for residential use when in fact the lots will not pass a soil suitability test for on-site sewage systems.

> **Example:** A broker is marketing a new condominium complex which is under construction. Acting with the full knowledge and consent of the broker, the broker's agents regularly inform prospective buyers that units will be available for occupancy on June 1, when in fact the units won't be available until at least September 1.

Conflict of Interest [G.S. 93A-6(a)(4) and (6); Rule A.0104(d)] and (i)

Undisclosed Dual Agency. G.S. 93A-6(a)(4) prohibits a real estate agent from *"acting for more than one party in a transaction without the knowledge of all parties for whom he or she acts."* Commission Rule A.0104(d) and (i) takes this a step further by providing that a broker or brokerage firm representing one party in a transaction shall not undertake to represent another party in the transaction without the express written authority (i.e., authorization of dual agency) of each party (subject to one exception, explained as part of the dual agency discussion in the "General Brokerage Provisions" section). A typical violation of this provision occurs when the agent has only one principal in a transaction but acts in a manner which benefits another party without the principal's knowledge. In such a situation, the agent violates the duty of loyalty and consent owed to his principal.

> **Example:** A house is listed with Firm X. When showing the house to a prospective buyer not represented by Firm X, an agent of Firm X advises the buyer to offer substantially less than the listing price because the seller must move soon and is very anxious to sell the property fast. The agent and Firm X are contractually obligated to represent only the seller. By advising the prospective buyer as indicated in this example, the agent is acting to benefit the buyer without the seller's knowledge and consent. This act violates both the License Law and the Law of Agency.

> **Example:** An agent with Firm Y assists her sister in purchasing a house listed with Firm X without advising Firm X or the seller of her relationship with the buyer. The agent is "officially" acting as a subagent of the seller in the transaction. In this situation, there is an inherent conflict of interest on the part of the agent. If the agent does not disclose her relationships to

both parties, then the agent violates both the License Law and Law of Agency. In fact, since her allegiance lies with her sister, the agent should instead act as a buyer's agent from the outset. The same would be true if the buyer were a close friend or business associate of the agent, or in any way enjoyed a special relationship to the agent which would clearly influence the agent to act in behalf of the buyer rather than the seller.

Self-dealing. G.S. 93A-6(a)(4) also prohibits any **"self-dealing"** on the part of an agent. For example, if an agent attempts to make a secret profit in a transaction where he is supposed to be representing a principal, then the agent violates this "conflict of interest" provision.

> **Example:** An agent lists a parcel of undeveloped property which is zoned for single-family residential use. The agent knows that this property is about to be rezoned for multi-family residential use, which will greatly increase the property's value. Rather than informing the seller of this fact, the agent offers to buy the property at the listed price, telling the seller that he wants to acquire the property as a long-term investment. The deal closes. Several months later, after the rezoning has been accomplished, the agent sells the property at a substantial profit.

Representing Another Broker without Consent. G.S. 93A-6(a)(6) prohibits a licensee from "representing or attempting to represent a real estate broker other than the broker by whom he or she is engaged or associated, without the express knowledge and consent of the broker with whom he or she is associated." While brokers may work for or be associated with more than one real estate company at the same time, *so long as* they have the express consent of all brokers-in-charge, provisional brokers may never engage in brokerage activities for more than one company at a time.

Improper Brokerage Commission [G.S. 93A-6(a)(5) and (9)]

A broker may NOT pay a commission or valuable consideration to any person for acts or services performed in violation of the License Law. [G.S. 93A-6(a)(9)] *This provision flatly prohibits a broker from paying an unlicensed person for acts which require a real estate license.* Following are examples of prohibited payments:

> **Example:** The payment by brokers of commissions to previously licensed sales associates who failed to properly renew their licenses for any acts performed after their licenses had expired. [Note that payment could properly be made for commissions earned while the license was on active status, even if the license is inactive or expired at time of payment. The determining factor is whether the license was on active status at the time all services were rendered which generated the commission?]

> **Example:** The payment of a commission, salary or fee by brokers to unlicensed employees or independent

North Carolina Real Estate License Law and Commission Rules

contractors (e.g., secretaries, "trainees" who haven't passed the license examination, etc.) for performing acts or services requiring a real estate license.

Example: The payment by licensees of a "finder's fee," "referral fee," "bird dog fee," or any other valuable consideration to unlicensed persons who find, introduce, or bring together parties to a real estate transaction. This is true even if the ultimate consummation of the transaction is accomplished by a licensee and even if the act is performed without expectation of compensation. Thus, a licensee may NOT compensate a friend, relative, former client or any other unlicensed person for "referring" a prospective buyer, seller, landlord or tenant to such licensee. This prohibition extends to "owner referral" programs at condominium or time share complexes and "tenant referral" programs at apartment complexes.

In addition, a *provisional* broker may NOT accept any compensation for brokerage services from anyone other than his employing broker or brokerage firm. Consequently, *a broker may not pay a commission or fee directly to a provisional broker of another broker or firm. Any such payment must be made through the provisional broker's employing broker or firm.* [G.S. 93A-6(a)(5)]

Note: *See also the discussion of Rule A.0109 on "Brokerage Fees and Compensation" under the subsequent section titled "General Brokerage Provisions."*

Unworthiness and Incompetence [G.S. 93A-6(a)(8)]

This broad provision authorizes the Real Estate Commission to discipline any licensee who, based on his or her conduct and consideration of the public interest, is found to be unworthy or incompetent to work in the real estate business. A wide range of conduct may serve as the basis for a finding of unworthiness or incompetence, including conduct which violates other specific provisions of the License Law or Commission rules. Here are a few examples of improper conduct which do not specifically violate another License Law provision but which might support a finding of unworthiness or incompetence.

1. Failure to properly complete (fill in) real estate contracts or to use contract forms which are legally adequate.
2. Failure to diligently perform the services required under listing contracts or property management contracts.
3. Failure to provide accurate closing statements to sellers and buyers or accurate income/expense reports to property owners.

Improper Dealing [G.S. 93A-6(a)(10)]

This broad provision prohibits a real estate licensee from engaging in "any other conduct [not specifically prohibited elsewhere in the License Law] which constitutes **improper, fraudulent or dishonest dealing**." The determination as to whether particular conduct constitutes "improper, fraudulent or dishonest dealing" is made by the Real Estate Com-

mission on a case-by-case basis. Therefore, a broad range of conduct might be found objectionable under this provision, depending on the facts in a case.

One category of conduct which violates this provision is any breach of the duty to exercise skill, care, and diligence in behalf of a client under the Law of Agency. (Note that other breaches of Agency Law duties constituting either a "misrepresentation or omission," a "conflict of interest" or a "failure to properly account for trust funds" are covered by other specific statutory provisions.)

Another category of conduct which violates this provision is any violation of the State Fair Housing Act. This is mentioned separately under the "Discriminatory Practices" heading.

Example: An agent assists a prospective buyer in perpetrating a fraud in connection with a mortgage loan application by preparing two contracts — one with false information for submission to the lending institution, and another which represents the actual agreement between seller and buyer. (This practice is commonly referred to as "dual contracting" or "contract kiting.")

Example: A broker lists a property for sale and agrees in the listing contract to place the listing in the local MLS, to advertise the property for sale, and to use his best efforts in good faith to find a buyer. The broker places a "For Sale" sign on the property, but fails to place the property in the MLS for more than 30 days and fails to otherwise advertise the property during the listing period. (The broker has failed to exercise reasonable skill, care and diligence in behalf of his client as required by the listing contract and the Law of Agency.)

Example: An agent is aware that the owners of a house listed with his company are out of town for the weekend, yet the agent gives a prospective buyer the house keys and allows such prospect to look at the listed house without accompanying the prospect. (The agent has failed to exercise reasonable skill, care and diligence in behalf of his client.)

Discriminatory Practices [G.S. 93A-6(a)(10); Rule A.1601]

Any conduct by a licensee that violates the provisions of the State Fair Housing Act is considered by the Commission to constitute "improper conduct" and to be a violation of the License Law.

Practice of Law [G.S. 93A-4(e); G.S. 93A-6(a)(11); Rule A.0111]

Real estate licensees may not perform for others any legal service described in G.S. 84-2.1 or any other legal service. Following are several examples of real estate-related legal services which licensees may NOT provide.

1. Drafting legal documents such as deeds, deeds of trust, leases and real estate sales contracts for others. Although licensees may "fill in" or "complete" pre-

North Carolina Real Estate License Law and Commission Rules

printed real estate contract forms which have been drafted by an attorney, they may NOT under any circumstances complete or fill in deed or deed of trust forms.

2. Abstracting or rendering an opinion on legal title to real property.

3. Providing "legal advice" of any nature to clients and customers, including advice concerning the nature of any interest in real estate or the means of holding title to real estate. (Note: Although providing advice concerning the legal ramifications of a real estate sales contract is prohibited, merely "explaining" the provisions of such a contract is not only acceptable, but highly recommended.)

Violating any Commission Rule [G.S. 93A-6-(a)(15)]

The law also has a "catch-all" provision that subjects a licensee to disciplinary action for violating any rule adopted by the Commission.

Note: The provisions of G.S. 93A-6(a)(12)-(14) are addressed elsewhere in these "Comments" under the "General Brokerage Provisions" section.

Other Prohibited Acts [G.S. 93A-6(b)]

In addition to those prohibited acts previously discussed, G.S. 93A-6(b) prescribes several other specific grounds for disciplinary action by the Commission, including:

1. Where a licensee has obtained a license by false or fraudulent representation (e.g., falsifying documentation of prelicensing education, failing to disclose prior criminal convictions, etc.).

2. Where a licensee has been convicted of, or pled guilty or no contest to, a number of listed misdemeanors or felonies plus any other offense that shows professional unfitness or involves moral turpitude that would reasonably affect the licensee's performance in the real estate business.

3. Where a broker's unlicensed employee, who is exempt from licensing under G.S. 93A-2(c)(6) (property management exception), has committed an act which, if committed by the broker, would have constituted a violation of G.S. 93A-6(a) for which the broker could be disciplined.

4. Where a licensee who is also licensed as an appraiser, attorney, home inspector, mortgage broker, general contractor, or another licensed profession or occupation has been disciplined for an offense under any law involving fraud, theft, misrepresentation, breach of trust or fiduciary responsibility, or willful or negligent malpractice..

Lastly, be aware that under (b)(3), licensees may be disciplined for violating any of the 15 provisions under subsection (a) when selling, buying, or leasing their own property.

GENERAL BROKERAGE PROVISIONS

Discussed below are selected Commission rules related to general brokerage.

Agency Agreements and Disclosure [G.S. 93A-13 and Rule A.0104

Provided below is a brief summary of the various provisions of the Commission's rule regarding agency agreements and disclosure. For a much more in-depth discussion of this rule and its application, the reader is referred to the Commission's *North Carolina Real Estate Manual.*

Agency Agreements. G.S. 93A-13 and Rule A.0104(a) requires all agency agreements for brokerage services (in both sales and lease transactions) to be in writing and signed by the parties thereto. Rule A .0104(a):

- Requires agency agreements with **property owners** (both sellers and lessors) of any type of property to be in writing prior to the broker providing any services;

- Allows an express **oral buyer/tenant agency agreement** from the outset of the relationship, *but the agreement must be reduced to writing no later than the time any party to the transaction makes an offer.* As a practical matter, this oral agreement needs to address all key aspects of the relationship, including agent compensation, authorization for dual agency, etc.

(Note: A buyer/tenant agency agreement must be in writing from the outset if it seeks to limit the buyer/tenant's right to work with other agents or binds the client to the agent for any definite time period. In other words, *an oral buyer/tenant agency agreement must be "non-exclusive" and must be for an indefinite period and terminable by the client at any time***.)**

Further, every **written** agency agreement of any kind must also:

- *Provide for its existence for a definite period of time* and terminate without prior notice at the expiration of that period. [Exception: an agency agreement between a broker and a landlord to procure tenants for the landlord's property may allow for automatic renewal so long as the landlord may terminate with notice at the end of any contract or renewal period.]

- *Contain the Rule A.0104(b) non-discrimination (fair housing) provision*, namely: "The broker shall conduct all brokerage activities in regard to this agreement without respect to the race, color, religion, sex, national origin, handicap or familial status of any party or prospective party." (This provision must be set forth in a clear and conspicuous manner which shall distinguish it from other provisions of the agency agreement.)

- *Include the license number of the individual licensee* who signs the agreement.

Allowing an agent to work with a buyer under an express *oral* buyer agency agreement is intended to address the problem of buyers being reluctant to sign a written buyer agency agreement at the outset of their relationship with a buyer agent. The idea underlying this approach is to allow an agent to work temporarily with a prospective buyer as a buyer's agent under an oral agreement while the agent establishes a rapport with the buyer that makes the buyer feel more comfortable with signing a written buyer agency agreement.

Although the rule allows oral buyer/tenant agency agreements until the point in time when any party is ready to make an offer, it nevertheless is highly advisable that agents have such agreements reduced to writing and signed by the buyer/tenant at the earliest possible time in order to avoid misunderstanding and conflict between the buyer/tenant and agent. Recall also that the agent must obtain a written buyer/tenant agency agreement from the client not later than the time either party to the transaction extends an offer to the other.

If the buyer will not sign a written buyer agency agreement prior to making or receiving an offer, then the agent may not continue to work with the buyer as a buyer's agent. Moreover, the agent may not begin at this point to work with the buyer as a seller's subagent unless the agent (1) fully advises the buyer of the consequences of the agent switching from buyer's agent to seller's agent (including the fact that the agent would have to disclose to the seller any information, including "confidential" information about the buyer, that might influence the seller's decision in the transaction), (2) obtains the buyer's consent, and (3) obtains the consent of the seller and listing firm, which is the seller's agent. The foregoing applies equally to brokers working with tenants as a tenant agent.

Agency Disclosure Requirement. While Rule A.0104(a) requires all agency agreements, whether for lease or sales transactions, to be in writing, the *Rule A.0104(c) agency disclosure requirement applies only to **sales** transactions. It requires licensees to provide prospective buyers and sellers, at "first substantial contact," with a copy of the **Working with Real Estate Agents** brochure, to review the brochure with them and then reach an agreement regarding their agency relationship.* The licensee providing the brochure should also include his/her name and license number on the brochure. Note that the obligation under this rule is not satisfied merely by handing the prospective seller or buyer the brochure to read. The agent is required to review the contents of the brochure with the prospective buyer or seller and then reach agreement with the prospective buyer or seller as to whether the agent will work with the buyer or seller as his/her agent or as the agent of the other party.

In the case of a prospective **seller**, the agent may either (1) act as the seller's agent, which is the typical situation and requires a written agreement from the outset of their relationship, or (2) work with the seller as a buyer's agent if the agent already represents a prospective buyer.

In the case of a prospective **buyer**, the agent may either (1) act as the buyer's agent under either an oral or written agreement as addressed in Rule A.0104(a), or (2) work with the buyer as a seller's agent, disclosure of which must be in writing from the outset.

Disclosure of Agency Status by Sellers' Agents and Subagents to Prospective Buyers: Paragraph (e) of Rule A.0104, like paragraph (c), requires a seller's agent or subagent in sales transactions to disclose his/her agency status in writing to a prospective buyer at the "first substantial contact" with the buyer. It is recommended that sellers' agents make this required written disclosure using the form provided for this purpose in the *Working with Real Estate Agents* brochure that must be provided to buyers (as well as to sellers) at first substantial contact. This form has a place for the buyer to acknowledge receipt of the brochure and disclosure of agency status, thereby providing the agent with written evidence of having provided the brochure and disclosure. The disclosure may, however, be made using a different form — *the most important point is that the disclosure be made in writing in a timely manner.* The reason for this requirement is that buyers tend to assume that an agent they contact to work with them in locating a property for purchase is "their" agent and working primarily in their interest. This may or may not be the case in reality. *The purpose of the disclosure requirement is to place prospective buyers on notice that the agent they are dealing with is NOT "their" agent before the prospective buyer discloses to the agent information which the buyer would not want a seller to know because it might compromise the buyer's bargaining position.*

Most frequently, **"first substantial contact"** will occur at the first "face-to-face" meeting with a prospective buyer. However, the point in time that "first substantial contact" with a prospective buyer occurs will vary depending on the particular situation and may or may not be at the time of the first or initial contact with the prospective buyer. Many first contacts are by telephone and do not involve discussions which reach the level that would require disclosure, although some initial phone contacts, especially those with out-of-town buyers, could reach this level.

"First substantial contact" occurs at the point in time when a discussion with a prospective buyer begins to focus on the buyer's specific property needs and desires or on the buyer's financial situation. Typically, that point in time is reached when the agent is ready to solicit information from the prospective buyer that is needed to identify prospective properties to show the buyer. Therefore, *an agent planning to work with a prospective buyer as a seller's agent or subagent should assure that disclosure of his/her agency status is made in writing to the prospective buyer prior to obtaining from the prospective buyer any personal or confidential information that the buyer would not want a seller to know.*

A few **examples of such personal or confidential information include:** *The maximum price a buyer is willing to pay for a property; the buyer's ability to pay more than the price offered by the buyer; or the fact that a buyer has a special interest in purchasing the seller's property rather than some other similar property.* In any event, the disclosure must be made pri-

North Carolina Real Estate License Law and Commission Rules

or to discussing with the prospective buyer his/her specific needs or desires regarding the purchase of a property. As a practical matter, this means the *disclosure will always need to be made prior to showing a property to a prospective buyer.* The best policy is to simply make the disclosure at the earliest possible time.

If first substantial contact occurs by telephone or by means of other electronic communication where it is not practical to provide written disclosure, the agent shall immediately disclose by similar means whom he/she represents and shall immediately, but in no event later than three days from the date of first substantial contact, mail or otherwise transmit a copy of the written disclosure to the buyer.

Disclosure of Agency Status by Buyers' Agents to Sellers or Sellers' Agents. Paragraph (f) of Rule A.0104 *requires a buyer's agent to disclose his/her agency status to a seller or seller's agent at the "initial contact" with the seller or seller's agent.* "Initial contact" will typically occur when a buyer's agent telephones or otherwise contacts the listing firm to schedule a showing. The initial disclosure may be oral, but a written confirmation of the previous oral disclosure must be made (except in auction sale transactions) no later than the time of delivery of an offer to purchase. The written confirmation may be (and usually is) included in the offer to purchase. In fact, Commission Rule A.0112(a)(19) requires that any preprinted offer to purchase and contract form used by an agent include a provision providing for confirmation of agency status by each real estate agent (and firm) involved in the transaction.

Consent to Dual Agency. Paragraph (d) of Rule A.0104 requires generally that an agent must obtain the written authority of all parties prior to undertaking to represent those parties as a dual agent. It is important to note that this requirement applies to all real estate transactions (sales and lease/rentals), not just sales transactions. [In sales transactions, this written authority to act as a dual agent is usually included in the listing and buyer agency contracts. If those contracts do not grant such authority, then the agent must have both the seller and buyer consent to the dual agency prior to beginning to act as a dual agent for both parties.]

Paragraph (d) of Rule A.0104 currently *requires written authority for dual agency from the formation of the relationship except situations where a buyer/tenant is represented by an agent working under an oral agency agreement as permitted by A.0104(a), in which case written authority for dual agency must be obtained no later than the time one of the parties represented by the agent working as a dual agent makes an offer to purchase, sell, rent, lease, or exchange real estate to the other party.* Thus, it is permissible for the agent to operate for a limited period of time under an oral dual agency agreement. It is very important to remember that G.S. 93A-6(a)(4) still requires agents to obtain the consent of all parties prior to beginning to act as a dual agent for those parties. Therefore, it is essential that agents electing to operate as a dual agent for a limited period of time without obtaining this authority

in writing still explain fully the consequences of their acting as a dual agent and obtain the parties' oral consent.

As a practical matter in sales transactions, agents will frequently have already obtained written authority to act as a dual agent for in-house sales transactions at the time the initial written listing or buyer agency agreement is executed. However, under Paragraph (a) of Rule A.0104, many buyer's agents may elect to work with their buyer clients for a period of time under an oral buyer agency agreement. Paragraph (d) permits such buyer's agents to also operate for a limited period of time as a dual agent under an oral agreement in order to deal with situations where a buyer client is interested in a property listed with the agent's firm. Note that, *although an oral dual agency agreement for a limited period of time is permitted by Commission rules, it is strongly recommended that agents have any dual agency agreement in writing from the outset of the dual agency arrangement.* This will provide the agent with some evidence that the matter of dual agency was discussed with the parties and that they consented to it. Such evidence could prove quite useful if a party later asserts that the agent did not obtain their consent for dual agency in a timely manner.

Auction Sales Exemption. Paragraph (g) of Rule A.0104 provides that the provisions of Paragraphs (c), (d) and (e) of the Rule shall not apply to real estate licensees representing sellers in auction sales transactions. Note that in auction sales, the real estate agents involved almost invariably work only as seller's agents and this fact is considered to be self-evident. Thus, there is no need for agents to distribute and review the *Working with Real Estate Agents* brochure, no need for disclosure of agency status by the seller's agents, and no dual agency. For the unusual situation where a buyer may be represented by an agent in an auction sale transaction, Paragraph (h) of Rule A.0104 provides that such a buyer's agent shall, no later than the time of execution of a written agreement memorializing the buyer's contract to purchase, provide the seller or seller's agent with a written confirmation that he/she represents the buyer.

Dual Agency Status of Firm. Paragraph (i) of Rule A.0104 codifies in the Commission's rules the common law rule that *a firm which represents more than one party in the same real estate sales transaction is a dual agent, and further states that the firm, through the brokers affiliated with the firm, shall disclose its dual agency to the parties.* In other words, dual agency is not limited to those situations where an individual agent is working with both a buyer client and seller client (or lessor and commercial tenant) in the same transaction. If one agent of a firm is working with a buyer client of the firm and another agent of the same firm is working with a seller client of the firm in a transaction involving the sale of the seller client's property to the buyer client, then the firm is a dual agent (as it holds both agency agreements). However, a firm functions through its employees, namely, its associated agents; thus, under the common law, whenever the firm is a dual agent of certain parties in a transaction, all licensees affiliated with that

North Carolina Real Estate License Law and Commission Rules

firm are also dual agents of those parties in that transaction.

Designated Agency. Paragraphs (j) - (m) of Rule A.0104 authorize real estate firms to engage in a form of dual agency practice referred to in the rule as "**designated agency**" in certain **sales transactions involving in-house dual agency**. *"Designated agency involves appointing or "designating" an individual agent(s) in a firm to represent only the interests of the seller and another individual agent(s) to represent only the interests of the buyer when a firm has an in-house dual agency situation.*

The principal advantage of the designated agency approach over the "standard" dual agency approach is that each of a firm's clients (seller and buyer) receive fuller representation by their designated agent. In the typical dual agency situation, client advocacy is essentially lost because the dual agent may not seek an advantage for (i.e., "advocate" for) one client to the detriment of the other client. The dual agent must remain completely neutral and impartial at all times. Designated agency returns "advocacy" to the services provided by the respective designated agents and allows them to more fully represent their respective clients.

Authority to practice designated agency must be in writing no later than the time a written dual agency agreement is required under A.0104(d). Additional required procedures for practicing designated agency are clearly spelled out in Paragraphs (j) - (m) and are not discussed further here. For more detailed coverage of dual and designated agency, the reader is once again referred to the Commission's *North Carolina Real Estate Manual.*

Dual Agency by Individual Agent. Paragraph (n) of Rule A.0104 authorizes individual agents representing both the buyer and seller in the same real estate sales transaction pursuant to a written dual agency agreement to include in the agreement a provision authorizing the agent not to disclose certain "confidential" information about one party to the other party without permission from the party about whom the information pertains. This provision is intended to allow individual dual agents to treat confidential information about their clients in a manner similar to that allowed for firms practicing designated agency.

Brokers As Parties to Transactions. There is an inherent conflict of interest presented by a broker representing the very party against whom the broker, as an interested party, is negotiating. Paragraph (o) of Rule A.0104 prohibits a broker who is selling property in which the broker has an ownership interest from representing a buyer of the property. Except that a broker who is selling commercial real estate, as defined in Rule .1802 of this Subchapter, in which the broker has less than 25% ownership interest may represent a buyer of that property if the buyer consents to the representation after full written disclosure of the broker's ownership interest. However, a firm listing a property owned by a broker affiliated with the firm may represent a buyer of that property so long as the individual broker representing the buyer does not have an ownership interest in the prop-

erty and the buyer consents to the representation after full disclosure. Paragraph (p) of Rule A.0104 prohibits a listing broker or firm from purchasing a property listed by that broker or firm unless they first disclose to the seller in writing that a potential conflict of interest exists and that the seller may want to seek independent counsel. Prior to the listing broker entering into a purchase contract, the individual listing broker and firm must either terminate the listing agreement or transfer the listing to another broker in the firm. Prior to the firm entering into a purchase contract, the listing broker and firm must disclose to the seller in writing that the seller has the right to terminate the listing. The broker or firm must terminate the listing upon the request of the seller.

Broker Name and Address [Rule A.0103]

A broker must notify the Commission in writing (may include online) within 10 days of each change in personal name, firm name, trade name, residence address and firm address, telephone number, and email address.

If a broker intends to advertise in any manner using a firm name or assumed name which does not set forth the surname of the broker, the broker must first register the firm name or assumed name with the county *register of deeds office in each county in which the broker intends to engage in brokerage activity* and must also notify the Commission of the use of such firm name or assumed name. For individuals and partnerships, a name is "assumed" when it does not include the surname of the licensee(s). For a firm required to be registered with the Secretary of State, a name is "assumed" when it is different from the firm's legal name as registered with the Secretary of State. Note: most franchisees operate under assumed names. An Assumed Name certificate can be filed in the Register of Deeds office for uploading to the statewide database maintained by the Secretary of State.

A licensee operating as a sole proprietorship, partnership or business entity other than a corporation or limited liability company may NOT include in its legal or assumed name the name of an unlicensed person or a provisional broker.

A broker who proposes to use a business name that includes the name of another active, inactive or cancelled broker must have the permission of that broker or his or her authorized representative. This rule provision is intended to prohibit a broker or firm from using without proper authorization the name of some other broker or former broker who is not currently associated with the broker or firm, such as a former associate or a deceased broker.

Advertising [Rule A.0105]

A licensee must have the proper authority to advertise. A broker may not advertise or display a "for sale" or "for rent" sign on a property without the written consent of the owner or the owner's authorized agent. A broker may not advertise any brokerage service for another without the consent of his or her broker-in-charge and without including in any advertisement the name of the firm or sole proprietorship with which the broker is associated.

The rule also prohibits any advertisement by a licensee that indicates an offer to sell, buy, exchange, rent or lease real property is being made by the licensee's principal without the involvement of a broker – i.e., a **"blind ad."** *All advertising by a licensee must indicate that it is the advertisement of a broker or brokerage firm.*

Delivery of Instruments [G.S. 93A-6(a); Rule A.0106]

Among other things, this rule, which implements G.S. 93A-6(a)(13), *requires agents to deliver to their customer or client copies of any required written agency agreement, contract, offer, lease, rental agreement, option or other related transaction document within three days of the broker's receipt* of the executed document. Regarding offers, this does NOT mean that agents may in every case wait up to three days to present an offer to a seller. Rather, it means that an agent must, as soon as possible, present to the seller any offer received by the agent. If the agent is the "selling agent," then the offer should be immediately presented to the "listing agent" who should, in turn, immediately present the offer to the seller. The "three-day" provision is included only to allow for situations where the seller is not immediately available (e.g., seller is out of town), and represents an outside time limit within which offers must always be presented. In all cases where the seller is available, the offer should be presented as soon as possible.

The same rule also means that a prospective buyer who signs an offer must immediately be provided a copy of such offer. (A photocopy is acceptable for this purpose.) Do NOT wait until after the offer is accepted (or rejected) by the seller.

In addition, this rule means that an offer must be immediately presented to a seller even if there is a contract pending on the property. Of course, in this instance, it is essential that the agent also advise the seller that serious legal problems could result from the seller's acceptance of such offer and that the seller should contact an attorney if he is interested in treating the offer as a "back-up" offer or in attempting to be released from the previously signed contract.

Copies of any signed sales contract or lease must also be promptly delivered to the parties within the three-day period. Clients should be provided a copy of the agency agreement upon signing, since both parties presumably are present, but certainly within three days of receipt by the broker.

Finally, G.S. 93A-6(a)(14) requires a broker to provide his/her client a detailed and accurate closing statement showing the receipt and disbursement of all monies relating to the transaction about which the broker knows or reasonably should know. A broker may rely on a closing statement prepared by an attorney but must review the statement for accuracy.

Retention of Records [Rule A.0108]

Brokers are required to retain records pertaining to their brokerage transactions for three years from the successful or unsuccessful conclusion of the transaction or the disbursement of all trust monies pertaining to that transaction, whichever occurs later. However, if the broker's agency agreement is terminated prior to the conclusion of the transaction, the broker shall retain transaction records for three years after the agency agreement is terminated or the disbursement of all funds held by or paid to the broker in connection with the transaction, whichever occurs later. Documents that must be retained include sale contracts, leases, offers (even those not accepted), agency contracts, earnest money receipts, trust account records, disclosure documents, closing statements, broker cooperation agreements, broker price opinions and comparative market analyses (including notes and supporting documentation), advertising, sketches, and any other records relating to a transaction.

Rule A .0108(d) also requires an individual broker to provide a copy of such records including written agency disclosures, agency agreements, and contracts to the firm or sole proprietorship with which they are affiliated within three days of the broker's receipt of such documents.

Brokerage Fees and Compensation [Rule A.0109]

This rule addresses various issues associated with the disclosure of and sharing of compensation received by a real estate licensee.

Disclosure to principal of compensation from a vendor or supplier of goods or services. Paragraph (a) prohibits a licensee from receiving any form of valuable consideration from a vendor or supplier of goods or services in connection with an expenditure made on behalf of the licensee's principal in a real estate transaction without first obtaining the written consent of the principal.

> **Example:** A broker manages several rental units for various owners and routinely employs Ajax Cleaning Service to clean the units after the tenants leave. The broker pays Ajax a $50 per unit fee for its services out of rental proceeds received and deposited in his trust account. Ajax then "refunds" to the broker $10 for each $50 fee it receives, but the property owners are not aware that the broker receives this payment from Ajax in addition to his regular brokerage fee. The broker in this situation is making a secret profit without the property owners' knowledge and is violating the rule.

Disclosure to a party of compensation for recommending, procuring or arranging services for the party. Paragraph (b) prohibits a licensee from receiving any form of valuable consideration for recommending, procuring, or arranging services for a party to a real estate transaction without full and timely disclosure to such party. The party for whom the services are recommended, procured, or arranged does not have to be the agent's principal.

> **Example:** An agent sells a listed lot to a buyer who wants to build a house on the lot. Without the buyer's knowledge, the agent arranges with ABC Homebuilders for ABC to pay the agent a 3% referral fee if the agent recommends ABC to the buyer and the buyer employs ABC to build his house. The agent then recommends ABC to the buyer, ABC builds the buyer's house for $100,000 and ABC secretly pays

North Carolina Real Estate License Law and Commission Rules

the agent $3,000 for his referral of the buyer. The agent has violated this rule. (Note that the buyer in this situation likely paid $3,000 more for his house than was necessary because it is very likely the builder added the agent's referral fee to the price he charged the buyer for building the house. The main point here is that the buyer had the right to know that the agent was not providing disinterested advice when recommending the builder.)

Example: A selling agent in a real estate transaction, while acting as a subagent of the seller, recommends to a buyer who has submitted an offer that the buyer apply to Ready Cash Mortgage Company for his mortgage loan. The agent knows that Ready Cash will pay him a "referral fee" of $100 for sending him the buyer's business if the loan is made to the buyer, but the agent does not disclose this fact to the buyer. If the agent subsequently accepts the referral fee from the lender, he will have violated this rule. (The buyer has the right to know that the agent's recommendation is not a disinterested one.)

Disclosure to principal of compensation for brokerage services in sales transactions. Paragraph (c) deals with disclosure to a licensee's principal of the licensee's compensation in a **sales** transaction from various sources other than in situations addressed in paragraphs (a) and (b). A broker may not receive any compensation, incentive, bonus, rebate or other consideration of more than nominal value (1) from his or her principal unless the compensation, etc. is provided for in a written agency contract or (2) from any other party or person unless the broker provides to his or her principal a full and timely disclosure of the compensation.

Example: ABC Homebuilders offers to pay any broker who procures a buyer for one of ABC's inventory homes a **bonus** of $1,000 that is in addition to any brokerage commission the broker earns under any agency contract and/or commission split agreements. Any broker working with a buyer-client who is considering the purchase of one of ABC's homes must comply with the disclosure requirement and disclose the bonus to the buyer in a timely manner. **Note:** If ABC Homebuilders also offers a bonus of $2,000 on a second sale of one of its homes and $3,000 on a third sale, and if a buyer's broker has already sold one of ABC's homes, then the broker must disclose to his or her buyer principal the entire bonus program and that his or her bonus will be at least $2,000 if the buyer purchases an ABC home.

Nominal compensation. Compensation is considered to be "nominal" if it is of insignificant, token or merely symbolic worth. The Commission has cited gifts of a $25 bottle of wine or a $50 dinner gift certificate as being examples of "nominal" compensation paid to a broker that do not require the consent of the broker's principal.

Full and timely disclosure. Paragraph (d) of Rule A.0109

explains what is meant by "full and timely disclosure" in paragraphs (a), (b) and (c). "Full" disclosure includes a description of the compensation, incentive, etc. including its value and the identity of the person or party by whom it will or may be paid. The disclosure is "timely" when it is made in sufficient time to aid a reasonable person's decision-making. In a sales transaction, the disclosure may be made orally, but must be confirmed in writing before the principal makes or accepts an offer to buy or sell.

Restrictions on compensation disclosure requirement. Paragraph (e) clarifies that a broker does NOT have to disclose to a person who is not his or her principal the compensation the broker expects to receive from his or her principal, and further clarifies that a broker does NOT have to disclose to his principal the compensation the broker expects to receive from the broker's employing broker/firm (i.e., the individual broker's share of the compensation paid to the broker's employing broker/firm).

Commission will not arbitrate commission disputes. G.S 93A-3(c) provides that the Commission shall not make rules or regulations regulating commission, salaries, or fees to be charged by licensees. Paragraph (f) of Rule A.0109 augments that statutory provision by providing that the Commission will not act as a board of arbitration regarding such matters as the rate of commissions, the division of commissions, pay of brokers and similar matters.

Compensation of unlicensed persons by brokers prohibited. G.S. 93A-6(a)(9) authorizes the Commission to take disciplinary action against a licensee for paying any person for acts performed in violation of the License Law. Paragraph (g) of Rule A.0109 simply augments this statutory provision by providing an affirmative statement that a licensee shall not in any manner compensate or share compensation with unlicensed persons or entities for acts performed in North Carolina for which a license is required. [Note that NC brokers may split commissions or pay referral fees to licensees of another state so long as the out-of-state licensee does not provide any brokerage services while physically in North Carolina.] One narrow, limited exception to this restriction is provided in Paragraph (h) – licensees may pay referral fees to travel agents who contact them to book vacation rentals only, so long as well-defined procedures are followed.

RESPA prohibitions control. Finally, Paragraph (i) of Rule A.0109 provides that nothing in this rule permits a licensee to accept any fee, kickback, etc. that is prohibited by the federal Real Estate Settlement Procedures Act (RESPA) or implementing rules, or to fail to make any disclosure required by that act or rules.

Broker-In-Charge [Rule A.0110].

Requirement to Have a Broker-In-Charge. Paragraph (a) of Rule A.0110 states the general rule that each real estate firm is required to have a broker designated by the Commission who meets the qualification requirements to serve as **"broker-in-charge"** of the firm's principal office and a different broker to serve in the same capacity at each branch office. It is important to note, as discussed previously under "License Requirement," that **"broker-in-charge"** *is not a separate license*, but only a separate license status category. No broker may be broker-in-charge of more than one office location at a time, and no office of a firm shall have more than one designated broker-in-charge. Rule A.0110(a) describes the lone exception in the rare circumstance when two or more firms share the same office space. Note that G.0103 defines the terms "office," "principal office" and "branch office" – these definitions are not repeated here.

Exception to BIC Requirement for Certain Firms.

Paragraph (c) of Rule A.0110 provides: A licensed real estate firm is not required to have a BIC if it: (1) has been organized for the sole purpose of receiving compensation for brokerage services furnished by its qualifying broker through another firm or broker; (2) is treated for tax purposes as a Subchapter S corporation by the U.S. Internal Revenue service; (3) has no principal or branch office; and (4) has no licensed or unlicensed person associated with it other than its qualifying broker.

Sole Proprietors.

In addition to each firm having to have a broker-in-charge for each office, *most broker-sole proprietors (including sole practitioners) also must be a broker-in-charge.*

Rule A.0110 (b) provides that a broker who is a **sole proprietor** shall designate himself or herself as a broker-in-charge if the broker: (1) engages in any transaction where the broker is required to deposit and maintain monies belonging to others in a trust account; (2) engages in advertising or promoting his or her services as a broker in any manner; OR (3) has one or more other brokers affiliated with him or her in the real estate business. Note, however, that maintenance of a trust account by a broker solely for holding residential tenant security deposits received by the broker on properties owned by the broker in compliance with G.S. 42-50 shall not, standing alone, subject the broker to the requirement to be designated as a broker-in-charge.

The most misunderstood of the three broker-in-charge triggering requirements for sole proprietors cited above is # (2): "... *engages in advertising or promoting his or her services as a broker in any manner.*" Acts of a sole proprietor that trigger the BIC requirement under # (2) include, but are not limited to: Placing an advertisement for his or her services as a broker in any form or any medium; distributing business cards indicating he or she is a real estate broker; orally soliciting the real estate business of others; or listing a property for sale (which inherently involves holding oneself out as a broker and advertising).

Therefore, *a broker-sole proprietor may lawfully provide only limited brokerage services without designating himself or herself as a BIC.* A couple of examples of *permissible* brokerage activities by a broker-sole proprietor who is NOT a designated BIC include receiving a referral fee from another broker or brokerage firm for referring business to the broker or firm or representing a relative or friend as a buyer's broker in a sales transaction provided the broker has not solicited the business, has not advertised or promoted his or her

services, and does not hold earnest money beyond the time it is required to be deposited in a trust account.

The practical effect of these requirements is that a broker who will be operating independently in most cases must also designate himself or herself as a BIC. The real significance of these requirements for a sole proprietor will be better understood when the qualification requirements to serve as a BIC are subsequently discussed.

Requirements for BIC-Eligible Status.

Paragraph (e) of Rule A.0110 states that, in order for a broker to be designated as a BIC for a sole proprietorship, real estate firm, or branch office, the broker must FIRST have BIC Eligible status. A broker must request BIC Eligible status on a form provided by the Commission.

The qualifying requirements for BIC Eligible Status, pursuant to paragraph (e) of Rule A.0110, are:

- Broker license must be on "active" status but NOT on "provisional" status. A provisional broker is ineligible to serve as broker-in-charge, as is a broker whose license is inactive or expired.

- Broker must have at least 2 years of full-time or 4 years of part-time real estate brokerage experience within the previous 5 years or be a North Carolina licensed attorney with a practice that consisted primarily of handling real estate closings and related matters in North Carolina for 3 years immediately preceding application. The requirement is for actual brokerage experience, not just having a license on "active" status. Note that by submission of the request form to the Commission, a broker certifies that he or she possesses the required experience. The Commission may at its discretion require the broker to provide evidence of possessing the required experience.

- After obtaining BIC Eligible status, a broker must complete the Commission's 12-hour Broker-In-Charge Course within 120 days of designation (unless the 12-hour course has been taken within the previous year). Failure to complete this course within 120 days will result in the broker losing BIC Eligible status. The broker must then take the course before he or she may again be granted BIC Eligible status.

Requesting Designation as Broker-in-Charge (BIC).

A broker who has BIC Eligible status may request BIC Designation on a form provided by the Commission at any time so long as the broker continuously maintains his/her BIC Eligible status. The broker may also request BIC Eligible status and BIC Designation simultaneously.

Broker-In-Charge (BIC) Duties.

The designated broker-in-charge is the primary person the Commission will hold responsible for the supervision and management of an office. See paragraph (g) of Rule A.0110 for a list of the specific responsibilities of a broker-in-charge.

Maintaining BIC Eligible Status.

To maintain BIC Eligible status, paragraph (g) of Rule A.0110 requires that a broker must:

North Carolina Real Estate License Law and Commission Rules

• Renew his or her broker license in a timely manner each license year and keep the license on active status at all times.

• Complete each license year the four-hour mandatory Broker-in-Charge Update Course (BICUP) as well as any approved four-hour CE elective.

The broker must begin taking the BICUP course during the same license year of designation, unless the broker completed the General Update (GENUP) course prior to designation.

The BICUP Course satisfies the broker's four-hour mandatory continuing education Update course requirement. If a broker with BIC Eligible status fails to take both the BICUP and one elective CE course by June 10 in any given year when required, then the broker will lost BIC Eligible status, and BIC designation if applicable, the following July 1.

Termination of BIC Eligible Status and Broker-In-Charge Designation. Paragraph (i) of Rule A.0110 provides that a broker's BIC Eligible status, and, if currently designated as a BIC, his or her BIC designation, shall be terminated if the broker: made any false statements or presented any false, incomplete, or incorrect information in connection with an application; fails to complete the 12-hour Broker-in-Charge Course pursuant to Paragraph (e) of the Rule; fails to timely renew his or her broker license, or the broker's license has been suspended, revoked, or surrendered; or fails to timely complete the Broker-in-Charge Update Course (BICUP) and a four credit hour elective course in any license year.

Regaining Lost BIC Eligible Status and BIC Designation. Pursuant to Rule A .0110(m), once a broker's BIC Eligible status has been terminated, the broker must complete the following steps in the order prescribed to regain the status:

1. The broker must first have a license on active status. If the license has expired, it must first be reinstated. If the license is inactive due to a CE deficiency, then the licensee must first complete whatever CE is necessary to reactivate the license and in either case, must then submit a reactivation form to the Commission requesting that the license be placed back on active status. A broker who has lost his or her BIC Eligible status should not take either the 12-hour BIC Course or the BICUP course prior to officially reactivating his/her license with the Commission.

2. Once back on active status, the broker must possess the experience required for initial designation and must first complete the 12-hour BIC Course prior to requesting BIC Eligible status and re-designation as a BIC regardless of when the broker may have previously taken the 12-hour course. There are no exceptions to this requirement to retake the 12-hour course prior to re-designation.

Notice to Commission When BIC Status Ends. A BIC must notify the Commission in writing within 10 days upon ceasing to serve as BIC of a particular office. [See Paragraph (g).]

Exception for certain Subchapter S corporations. See Paragraph (c).

Nonresidents. Nonresident individuals and firms holding a NC broker and/or firm license and engaging in brokerage activity in NC are subject to the same requirements as NC resident brokers/firms with regard to when they must have a designated broker-in-charge. Thus, a nonresident company engaging in brokerage in NC must have a broker-in-charge of the company who holds an active NC broker license for purposes of its NC business, although the office need not be physically located in North Carolina. Similarly, a nonresident NC broker sole practitioner engaging in activity that triggers the broker-in-charge requirement for a resident NC broker sole practitioner (see previous discussion on this subject) also must be designated as a broker-in-charge for NC brokerage purposes as without a BIC, a company has no office anywhere.

Education Exception for Certain Nonresident NC Brokers-In-Charge: A nonresident NC broker who has attained BIC Eligible status and been designated as the broker-in-charge of an office NOT located in NC and who has no office, primary residence or mailing address in North Carolina is NOT required to complete four-hour mandatory Broker-in-Charge Update (BICUP) Course to maintain BIC Eligible status. [See Rule 58A .1711.] However, a nonresident broker who has attained BIC-Eligible status IS REQUIRED to complete the 12-hour BIC Course pursuant to paragraph (e) of Rule A .0110.

Drafting Legal Instruments [Rule A.0111]

This rule prohibits licensees from drafting legal instruments, e.g., contracts, deeds, deeds of trust, etc., but does allow them to fill in the blanks on preprinted sales or lease contract forms, which is not construed to be the unauthorized practice of law.

Offers and Sales Contracts [Rule A.0112]

This rule specifies what minimum terms must be contained in any preprinted offer or sales contract form a licensee, acting as an agent, proposes for use by a party in a real estate transaction.

Reporting Criminal Convictions [Rule A.0113]

Licensees are required to report to the Commission any criminal convictions for a felony or misdemeanor, any disciplinary action taken against them by any other occupational licensing board, or any restriction, suspension or revocation of a notarial commission within sixty (60) days of the final judgment or order in the case. This reporting requirement is ongoing in nature. *Note that Driving While Impaired (DWI) is a misdemeanor and must be reported!*

Residential Property and Owners' Association Disclosure Statement [Rule A.0114]

State law (Chapter 47E of the General Statutes) requires that most residential property owners complete a disclosure form to give to prospective purchasers. The form seeks to elicit information about the condition of the property by asking various questions, to which owners may answer "yes," "no," or "no representation." Failure to provide a buyer with this form may allow the buyer to cancel the contract by notifying the seller in writing within three calendar days of contract acceptance.

Note: Licensees in residential real estate transactions have a duty under G.S. 47E-8 to inform their clients of the client's rights and obligations under the statute. The Real Estate Commission also views the Real Estate License Law as imposing on licensees working with sellers and buyers certain additional responsibilities to ensure statutory compliance and serve their clients' interests. Licensees are expected to "assist" sellers with completion of the form but should not complete the form for a seller or advise a seller as to what representation (or No Representation) to make. That being said, licensees should be certain to advise sellers that the licensee is obligated by law to disclose all material facts about or relating to the seller's property to prospective buyers regardless of what representation the seller makes on the disclosure form. See the Commission's *North Carolina Real Estate Manual* for a full discussion of the disclosure law and an agent's duties.

Sellers must also provide a Mineral and Oil and Gas Mandatory Disclosure Statement (MOGS) to buyers prior to making an offer to purchase and contract. The form has been developed by the Real Estate Commission and is available for download from the Commission's website, www.ncrec.gov. It is a separate form and is in addition to the Residential Property and Owner's Association Statement. A disclosure statement is not required for some transaction. For a complete list of exemptions, see G.S. 47E-2.

Broker's Responsibility for Closing Statements [G.S. 93A-6(a)(14)

The cited statute requires a broker, "…at the time a sales transaction is consummated, to deliver to the broker's client a detailed and accurate closing statement showing the receipt and disbursement of all monies relating to the transaction about which the broker knows or reasonably should know." The statute goes on to provide that if a closing statement is prepared by an attorney or lawful settlement agent, a broker may rely on the delivery of that statement, but *the broker must review the statement for accuracy and notify all parties to the closing of any errors.* Since virtually every residential transaction in North Carolina is closed by an attorney (or lawful settlement agent), it is standard practice for brokers to adopt the attorney's settlement statement to satisfy this License Law requirement.

Commission Guidelines. A settlement statement is a detailed report of all monies received and disbursed by the settlement agent in connection with a real estate sales transaction. It is essential that the settlement statement be accurate and that a copy be provided to each party. The settlement statement is prepared by the settlement agent – the individual conducting the closing, which in North Carolina is

almost always the closing attorney or a nonlawyer assistant working under the supervision of the closing attorney.

The TRID (Tila-RESPA Integrated Disclosures) rule became effective October 3, 2015, and applied to loan applications received on or after October 3, 2015. The TRID rule replaced the HUD-1 settlement statement (RESPA) and final Truth-in-Lending statement (TILA) with two Closing Disclosure (CD) documents, one for the borrower and a separate one for the seller. Closing disclosures are disclosures only and are not equivalent to a settlement statement. While the HUD-1 is no longer used in TRID-governed transactions, other types of settlement statements may be used, such as settlement/closing statements created and published by the American Land Title Association (ALTA). Also, the HUD-1 may be used as the settlement statement in non-TRID-governed transactions, such as cash transactions, construction loans, or purchases of investment property.

The Commission has published in its North Carolina Real Estate Manual the following guidelines regarding brokers' responsibilities for settlement statements:

- A broker must confirm the accuracy of all entries about which s/he has direct knowledge. Such items include, but may not be limited to: the sale price; amount of the due diligence fee and earnest money deposit; amount of the brokerage commission and split; any amounts due either party under the offer to purchase and contract, e.g., closing costs paid by seller, as well as any sums paid by or due to third parties related to the transaction, if the broker knows or should know about the expense.

- As to amounts paid by or due to third parties, brokers generally may assume that the amounts for charges and fees as stated on the settlement statement are correct unless there is something that would lead a reasonable broker to suspect that an amount is incorrect. As to all debits and credits related to the transaction, whether paid before or at closing, the broker must:

  1) review and confirm that all charges and credits have been properly debited or credited to the seller or buyer and are entered in the correct column; and

  2) review and confirm the accuracy of the calculations for all prorated items, escrow reserves, interim interest, excise tax and the "bottom line figures," i.e., total settlement charges to each party, cash from borrower-buyer, and cash to seller.

- If a broker is aware of any expense related to the transaction paid to or by either party or any third party that is not included on the settlement statement, the broker must notify both the settlement agent and the lender of the omission, as the settlement statement should reflect all expenses and payments related to the transaction, not just monies the settlement agent

North Carolina Real Estate License Law and Commission Rules

disburses.

- A broker should notify the settlement agent if the broker believes there are any errors or omissions on the statement.

HANDLING TRUST FUNDS

This section addresses those aspects of handling trust funds that are taught in the Real Estate Broker Pre-licensing Course and tested on the real estate license examination for entry-level brokers. All brokers are encouraged to take the Basic Trust Account course for a fuller treatment of this subject. The Basic Trust Account course schedule is available on the Commission's website at www.ncrec.gov.

Definition of Trust Money

In the context of real estate transactions, "**trust money**" is most easily defined as *money belonging to others received by a real estate broker who is acting **as an agent** in a real estate transaction*. It is *also any money held by a licensee who acts as the temporary custodian of funds belonging to others*. Such money must be held in trust even if the circumstances are only collateral to the licensee's role as an agent in a real estate related matter, e.g., a listing agent receives monies from his out of town seller for yard maintenance while the property is being marketed. The most common examples of trust money are:

- Earnest money deposits
- Down payments
- Tenant security deposits
- Rents
- Homeowner association dues and assessments, and
- Money received from final settlements

In the case of resort and other short-term rentals, trust money also includes:

- Advance reservation deposits
- State (and local, if applicable) sales taxes on the gross receipts from such rentals

Trust or Escrow Account [G.S. 93A-6(a)(12) & (g); 93A-45(c); Rule A.0116, .0117]

One of the most basic tenets of broker accountability when handling trust money is that it must be deposited into a trust or escrow account as described below. A "trust account" or "escrow account" (the terms are synonymous for Commission purposes) is simply a bank account into which trust money (and *only* trust money) is deposited. The three primary features of a trust or escrow account are that it is:

1) **separate**, containing only monies belonging to others,
2) **custodial**, meaning *only the broker or the broker's designated employee has disbursement control over the account*, but no one who has funds in the account has that ability, **and**
3) **available on demand**, that is, the funds may be withdrawn at any time without prior notice.

Type and Location of Trust Account. A broker's trust account or escrow account must be:

1) a demand deposit account
2) in a federally insured depository institution
3) lawfully doing business in North Carolina
4) that agrees to make the account records available for inspection by Commission representatives. [G.S. 93A-6(g)]

Thus, for the purpose of holding most trust money, the bank can be located outside North Carolina if the foregoing conditions are met.

Designation of Trust Account and FDIC Insurance. A broker-in-charge who must maintain a trust account must ensure that the bank properly designates the account and that the words "trust account" or "escrow account" appear on all signature cards, bank statements, deposit tickets and checks. Even though the escrow account typically is in the name of the company or broker, so long as the broker properly designates the account as a "trust" or "escrow" account and keeps accurate records that identify each owner of the funds and/or depositor (buyer, seller, lessor, lessee, etc.), the depositors are protected from the funds being "frozen" or attached if the broker/trustee becomes insolvent, incapacitated, dies, has tax liens, becomes involved in a lawsuit, etc. Failure to properly designate an account titled in the name of the company/broker as a trust or escrow account may result in attachment of the account by others to collect a judgment or denial of FDIC insurance coverage as to each individual's interest in the account.

So long as the account is properly designated as a trust/escrow account, *all deposits are insured by the Federal Deposit Insurance Corporation (FDIC) up to $250,000 **per each individual** for whom funds are held*. Thus, a broker's trust account may contain $500,000 total, but *all funds are fully insured so long as no one individual's interest in the account exceeds $250,000*. (**Note**, however, that an individual still may be underinsured if the individual maintains accounts in his/her individual name at the same financial institution as the broker's trust/escrow account.)

When a Trust Account Is Required. A broker must open and maintain a trust account when the broker or any affiliated licensee takes possession of trust money. A broker who is inactive or otherwise not using his/her real estate license is not required to open or maintain a trust account because s/he should not be engaged in brokerage nor receiving monies belonging to others. Similarly, if an *active* practicing broker does not collect or otherwise handle the funds of others, no trust account is required. Note: A broker who leases residential property he or she owns to tenants may be required to maintain a trust account under 42-50 NC Residential Landlord Tenant law.

Number of Trust Accounts. Except for brokers who are managing homeowner or property owner association funds, a broker holding trust money is only required to have one trust account. All earnest money deposits, tenant security deposits, rents, and other trust monies may be deposited into this one common trust account. However, brokers who are active in both sales and property management often find it helpful to use more than one trust account. For example, they may wish to keep a "general sales trust account" for earnest money deposits, settlement proceeds, etc., and a "rental trust account" for tenant security deposits, rents, and related receipts. Although it is not required, many brokers involved in property management and leasing elect to maintain an additional "security deposit trust account" to keep tenant security deposits separate from rents and other related receipts. However, **Rule A.0118(a)** requires brokers who handle homeowner or property owner association funds to maintain a *separate trust account for each property owner association or homeowner association they manage*. The funds of one homeowner association are not to be commingled with funds from any other association nor with any general trust monies. The broker also must provide the association with periodic written statements not less than once each quarter reporting all monies received, disbursed, and due, but not paid (i.e., delinquent), as well as the balance of funds in the account.

"Commingling" Prohibited. [G.S. 93A-6(a)(12)] The basic statutory provision relating to a licensee's handling of the money or property of others states that a broker may not "commingle" his or her own money or property with the money or property of others. This means that a broker may not maintain funds belonging to others in the same bank account that contains his or her personal or business funds. Funds belonging to others must be held in a trust account and, except as described below regarding "bank service charges on trust accounts," a broker may not deposit his or her own funds in that trust account. The prohibition against commingling also means, for example, that a broker who has an ownership interest in property is precluded from depositing monies (e.g., earnest money, rent, security deposits, etc.) related to that property in his brokerage trust account.

Bank Service Charges on Trust Accounts. Trust accounts usually are subject to the same service charges as regular checking accounts. Whenever possible, brokers should arrange for the depository/bank either to bill the broker for these expenses or charge these expenses to the broker's personal or general operating account. However, if such arrangements cannot be made, the Commission will permit a broker to deposit and maintain in his trust account a maximum of $100.00 of his personal funds (or such other amount as may be required) to cover (not avoid) such charges. So, if a broker's monthly service charges and other fees typically are $100, then the broker may deposit up to $200 of his/her own money to *cover* these charges. A broker who deposits any of his/her own money in the trust account to cover bank charges must be careful to properly enter and identify these personal funds in his/her trust account records by use of a personal funds ledger. While this technically constitutes "commingling," it is permissible commingling to avoid the greater evil of using other people's money

to pay these bank charges.

Interest-Bearing Trust Account. Both G. S. 93A-6(a)(12) and Rule A.0116(c) permit a broker to deposit trust money into an interest-bearing trust account so long as the broker first obtains written authorization for deposit in an interest-bearing account from all parties having an interest in the monies being held. Such authorization must specify how and to whom the interest will be paid. If the authorization is contained in an offer, contract, lease or other transaction instrument, it must be set forth in a conspicuous manner that distinguishes it from other provisions of the instrument. Remember, however, that all trust accounts must be a *demand account*, so investment of trust monies in any type of security, such as a government bond or a fixed term certificate of deposit, is prohibited.

Broker-In-Charge Responsible for Trust Accounts. [Rule A.0117; Rule A.0110(g)(4)] Rule A.0117(a) requires a broker to maintain complete records showing the deposit, maintenance and withdrawal of money belonging to the broker's principals or *held in escrow or in trust for the broker's principals*. Paragraph (h) of that rule also provides that the Commission may inspect trust account records periodically without prior notice and whenever the records are pertinent to investigation of a complaint against a licensee. Rule A.0110(g)(4) refines this requirement by specifying that a **broker-in-charge (BIC)** *is responsible for the proper maintenance of real estate trust accounts and records pertaining thereto*.

Custodian of Trust Account Records Other Than the Broker-In-Charge. While a broker-in-charge may transfer possession of trust money to a bookkeeper, secretary, or some other clerical employee to record and deposit the funds in a trust account and to maintain trust account records, the broker-in-charge nonetheless remains responsible for the care and custody of such funds. Brokers-in-charge should closely and diligently supervise the acts of all persons having access to the trust account, since final accountability for the accuracy and integrity of the account rests with the broker-in-charge. *Access to trust money should be limited and carefully controlled.*

Disbursement of Earnest Money [Rule A0116(e)] This rule permits a broker-in-charge to transfer an earnest money deposit from his/her trust account to the closing attorney or other settlement agent not more than ten (10) days prior to the anticipated settlement date. Earnest money may **not** be disbursed prior to settlement for any other purpose without the written consent of the parties. Thus, earnest money may not be used by the broker to pay for inspection reports or other services on behalf of the buyer prior to settlement without the written consent of the seller, and vice-versa.

Disputed Trust Funds. Rule A.0116(d) addresses disputed trust funds as follows: "In the event of a dispute between buyer and seller or landlord and tenant over the return or forfeiture of any deposit other than a residential tenant security deposit held by a broker, the broker shall retain said deposit in a trust or escrow account until the broker has

North Carolina Real Estate License Law and Commission Rules

obtained a written release from the parties consenting to its disposition or until disbursement is ordered by a court of competent jurisdiction." The rule also references the G.S. 93A-12 procedures for depositing disputed funds with the Clerk of Court as well as when one party abandons his or her claim to the disputed funds. However, these procedures are beyond the scope of these materials and are more important for brokers-in-charge to know.

Handling of Trust Money [Rule A.0116(a), (b) & (g)]

The **general rule** is that all trust monies received by a licensee must be deposited in a trust account **within three banking days of receipt**. **Exception: Earnest money** received with offers to purchase and **tenant security deposits** in connection with leases must be deposited in a trust account *not later than three banking days following* **acceptance** *of the offer to purchase or lease agreement* **unless** the deposit is tendered in *cash* in which event it must be deposited within *three banking days following* **receipt**, *even if the contract or lease has not been accepted*. In part, this is because cash is immediately available and may be refunded within a day of deposit, unlike checks which may require a few days to clear.

Understand that a broker *may* choose to immediately deposit a check received for an earnest money deposit or tenant security deposit and is *not required* to wait until contract acceptance unless so instructed by the buyer/tenant. Of course, early deposit may cause problems if the offer to purchase or lease is not accepted and the prospective buyer or tenant understandably wants their deposit to be immediately returned. The date of acceptance should be shown in the purchase or lease agreement to determine when the three banking days begins.

Receipt of Trust Money by Provisional Broker. [Rule A.0116(b)(1)&(2), Rule A.1808.] *All trust money received by a* **provisional broker** *must be delivered immediately to the provisional broker's broker-in-charge.* In other words, provisional brokers may not retain or hold trust money any longer than absolutely necessary to deliver the trust money to his/her broker-in-charge. Similarly, trust monies received by a **nonresident limited commercial broker** are to be delivered immediately to and held by the resident North Carolina broker with whom the nonresident is affiliated. Brokers-in-charge should have written policies that clearly state the procedures to be followed when *any agent* affiliated with the company, whether a provisional or non-provisional broker, receives trust monies.

Handling Option Money and Due Diligence Fee. Rule A.0116(b)(4) states in part: "A broker may accept custody of a **check or other negotiable instrument** *made payable to the seller* of real property as payment for an **option** or **due diligence fee**, but only for the purpose of delivering the instrument to the seller. While the instrument is in the custody of the broker, the broker shall, according to the instructions of the buyer, either deliver it to the seller or return it to the buyer. The broker shall safeguard the instrument and shall be responsible to the parties on the instrument for its safe delivery as required by this Rule. A broker shall not retain such an instrument for more than three business days

after the acceptance of the option or other sales contract."

The rule is basically self-explanatory. In the rule, "custody" means possession. Recall that option money or a due diligence fee is paid directly to the seller, to whom the check is written as payee, and so it is not appropriate for a broker to deposit these checks into his/her trust account because the check is not payable to the broker or real estate company as is the case with earnest money checks. Either the listing agent or buyer's agent may hold the check or negotiable instrument until negotiations are completed and a contract is formed, at which point the check should be delivered to the seller as soon as possible.

If, however, a buyer for some reason gives a broker *cash for the option money or due diligence fee*, then the broker must *immediately deposit the cash in his/her trust account* pending contract formation as *cash must* **always** *be deposited into a trust account within* **three banking days of receipt** — *no exceptions*. If the parties enter into a contract, then the broker would write a check from the trust account payable to the seller, noting in the memo section and trust account records that it is for the option fee or due diligence fee from the buyer.

Safeguarding Trust Money; Improper Use of Trust Money. [Rule A.0116(g)]

This rule places on *every licensee* the responsibility to safeguard the money or property of others coming into his or her possession according to the requirements of the License Law and Commission rules. In addition, it states that: "A broker shall not convert the money or property of others to his or her own use, apply such money or property to a purpose other than that for which it was intended or permit or assist any other person in the conversion or misapplication of such money or property."

BROKER PRICE OPINION AND COMPARATIVE MARKET ANALYSIS
[G.S. 93A, Article 6; Commission Rules Chapter 58A, Section .2200]

Definitions. General Statute §93A-82 of the North Carolina Real Estate License Law and General Statute §93E-1-4(7c) of the North Carolina Appraisers Act both define a **"broker price opinion"** (**"BPO"**) and a **"comparative market analysis"** (**"CMA"**) as "…an estimate prepared by a licensed real estate broker that details the probable selling price or leasing price of a particular parcel of or interest in property and provides a varying level of detail about the property's condition, market, and neighborhood, and information on comparable properties, but does not include an automated valuation model." Thus, *the terms "BPO" and "CMA" have exactly the same legal meaning* even though an estimate provided for a seller or buyer client or prospective client is most commonly referred to as a CMA and an estimate performed for a third party for a purpose other than mortgage loan origination (for example, a foreclosure or short sale decision) is typically referred to as a BPO.

- A "non-provisional" broker with a current license on "active" status may prepare a broker price opinion

(BPO) or comparative market analysis (CMA) for a fee for a variety of persons and entities for a variety of reasons, not just for actual or prospective brokerage clients. Note, however, that a provisional broker may NOT perform a BPO or CMA for a fee for anyone. [G.S. §93A-83(a) and (b)]

- A broker may **NOT** prepare a BPO (or CMA) for an existing or potential lienholder or other third party where the BPO is to serve as the basis to determine the **value** of a property *for the purpose of originating a mortgage loan*, including first and second mortgages, refinances or equity lines of credit. [G.S. §93A-83(b)(6)]

- A BPO or CMA may only estimate the *"probable selling price"* or *"probable leasing price"* of a property, not the "value" of a property. Moreover, if a BPO or CMA does propose to estimate the "value" or "worth" of a property, it shall be legally considered a "real estate appraisal" that may only be prepared by a licensed or certified real estate appraiser, not by a real estate broker. [G.S. §93A-83(f)]

- A BPO or CMA provided *for a fee* must be performed in accordance with the requirements of Article 6 of the Real Estate License Law and standards set forth in rules adopted by the North Carolina Real Estate Commission. [Rules, Ch. 58, Section A.2200]

- A BPO or CMA must be *in writing* and must address those matters specifically required by the statute or Commission rule. [G.S. §93A-83(c)]

Standards for BPOs and CMAs Performed for Compensation. Article 6 of the Real Estate License Law provides a number of standards that must be followed when a broker is performing a BPO/CMA for a fee. Additionally, the Commission has adopted rules (Section A.2200) setting forth specific standards for brokers when performing such standards. A broker performing a BPO/CMA utilizes the same valuation concepts and methodology as an appraiser performing an appraisal; however, the analysis associated with a BPO/CMA is less comprehensive and detailed than with an appraisal, and the regulatory standards for brokers performing BPOs/CMAs are less stringent than those required for real estate appraisers performing appraisals. [See G.S. 93A-83 and especially Commission Rule 58A.2202.]

Reporting Probable Selling/Leasing Price as a "Range." In recognition of the fact that brokers performing BPOs/CMAs are not expected to be as precise in their analysis and adjustments to comparable properties as an appraiser when performing an appraisal, the Commision's rules permit reporting in a BPO/CMA of probable selling price or leasing price (lease rate) as either a single figure or as a **price range.** The applicable rules also states: "When the estimate states a price range and the higher figure exceeds the lower figure by more than ten (10%), the broker shall include an explanation as to why the variance is more than 10 percent. [Rule A.2202(h)]

Use of Income Analysis Methodology Now Required Where Appropriate. The revised statutes eliminated the old Appraisers Act restriction that a broker's CMA for actual or prospective clients *and for compensation* was permitted only if the sales comparison approach was the only method used to derive an indication of the probable sales price. A broker performing a BPO or CMA to determine an estimated *"probable selling price or leasing price"* is now *required* to utilize methods involving the analysis of income where appropriate (i.e., income capitalization or gross rent multiplier methodology for income-producing properties) as well as the sales comparison method. [G.S. §93A-83(c)(3) and Commission Rule A.2202(e)]

Competence to Perform BPO/CMA. Although Article 6 of the License Law and Section A.2200 of the Commission's rules do not specifically require a broker to perform a BPO/CMA in **competent** manner, the reader should remember that the License Law has always made incompetence a basis for disciplinary action and those provisions also apply to the performance of BPOs and CMAs. If a broker is not qualified by way of education and experience to properly utilize the appropriate methodology required for a particular property (for example, income capitalization for a commercial property), then the broker is expected to decline the assignment.

CMAs/BPOs Performed for NO FEE. Any broker *(non-provisional or provisional)* has always been permitted to perform a BPO/CMA for any party when NO FEE is charged, and this continues to be the case under the revised law and rules. Note that *the Commission does not consider compensation of a broker for general brokerage services under a brokerage agreement to constitute a "fee" under Article 6 of N.C.G.S. §93A.* "General brokerage services" means services provided under a brokerage agreement to property owners in connection with listing/selling/leasing property and to prospective buyers or tenants in connection with purchasing or leasing a property. Such services include the provision by a licensee of a CMA or BPO. Similarly, the possibility of entering into a brokerage agreement (and earning a brokerage fee) does not constitute a "fee" when a licensee performs a CMA/BPO for a *prospective* client without charging a fee for the CMA/BPO. *It is important for licensees to remember, however, that the Commission expects every CMA/BPO performed by a licensee to be performed in a competent manner and without any undisclosed conflict of interest, even if no fee is received for the CMA/BPO. Thus, as a practical matter, a licensee performing a CMA/BPO for no fee should still look to the standards described in Commission Rule 58A .2202 for guidance regarding the proper performance of a CMA/BPO.*

For a full explanation of the law and rules governing BPOs and CMAs, and a Sales Comparison Analysis Illustration, the reader is referred to the Commission's *North Carolina Real Estate Manual,* which may be ordered through the Commission's website at www.ncrec.gov.

Practice Exam 1 Questions

1. Which of the following statements is true regarding Ad Valorem taxation in NC?

    1. Real property is taxed according to its most recent sale price.
    2. The Machinery Act requires reassessments for tax purposes every 4 years.
    3. Real property taxes and special assessments constitute an involuntary lien against property on Jan 1st of the tax year.
    4. Tax rates are effective until the next revaluation year.

2. John recently retired and moved to a coastal community located in North Carolina. He decides to seek opportunities to supplement his retirement income by responding to an advertisement to become a time share salesman. John is told by the developer that no license is required to sell a time share as he will be paid a flat fee for each time share sold. Is the developer correct?

    1. No. In order to sell time shares an individual will need to obtain a time share salesman license.
    2. No. In order to sell time shares an individual will need to obtain a North Carolina real estate license.
    3. Yes. So long as an individual is not paid a percentage based commission there is no requirement to obtain a time share salesman license.
    4. Yes. Time share sales fall under vacation property sales and therefore are exempt from the typical licensing requirement.

3. Which of the following statements regarding real estate sales contracts is TRUE?

    1. A provisional broker acting as the seller's agent is required to safeguard an option money check until effective and then must deliver it directly to the seller.
    2. An agent representing a buyer must submit an offer to purchase to the seller or seller's agent immediately or no later than 7 days.
    3. When earnest money is paid with an effective contract it must be deposited within 5 banking days of receipt.
    4. A broker is not permitted to accept an earnest money deposit if it is tendered in cash.

4. All of the following statements are true regarding a broker-in-charge, *EXCEPT*:

   1. A brokerage operating as a sole proprietorship must appoint a broker-in-charge in order to handle trust funds and advertise property.
   2. A broker-in-charge must notify the Commission when a change in his/her status occurs.
   3. A broker-in-charge is responsible for maintaining transaction records and notification of a change in address of the firm to the Commission.
   4. A broker-in-charge has a duty to supervise all brokers affiliated with the firm with regard to violations of license law.

5. A buyer's agent is responsible for which of the following in regard to the Closing Disclosure?

   1. The accuracy of all items on the Closing Disclosure.
   2. The accuracy of all items for buyer which they are reasonably aware.
   3. The correct distribution of proceeds of sale.
   4. To ensure that buyer has title insurance coverage.

6. A residential tenant in NC complains of a defect with the heating system in his unit. The heating system is not operating and the February temperatures are falling into the low 20's at night. Which of the following statements is most accurate?

   1. The tenant may vacate after providing written notice to the landlord and waiting a reasonable period of time.
   2. The tenant can make the repair and reduce rent by that amount.
   3. The tenant may remove himself from the property however must continue to pay the rent until a court order is obtained.
   4. The tenant may withhold rent in a designated account until work is done.

7. A landlord hires a broker to manage his residential rental units. The landlord requests that several provisions be added to the standard lease provided by the Realtor Association. Which of the following is NOT an acceptable suggestion by the agent?

   1. That the agent will write up a provision but only if the landlord dictates the language.
   2. The landlord may draft a provision for inclusion in the lease agreement.
   3. The landlord should seek legal advice regarding the language to be drafted in the contract.
   4. The Landlord and tenant may agree to anything in the lease that does not violate public policy.

8. Which of the following would most likely be included in the heated living area of a single family home?

   1. An in-law cottage that attaches to the house by an unheated breezeway
   2. A 2-car garage with finished, sheetrocked walls
   3. A finished walk-up attic with a maximum ceiling height of 6 foot 4 inches.
   4. A finished and heated basement accessible from the kitchen by interior stairs.

9. An engaged couple purchases a home to live in after they are married. They give no guidance to the attorney as to the nature of the deed. How will they hold title to the property once they are married?

   1. Tenants by Entirety
   2. Tenants in Common
   3. Joint Tenancy
   4. Severalty

10. Which is true regarding an agent's obligation for the Residential Property Owners Association Disclosure Statement?

    1. The agent should advise the seller on how to answer a specific question, as the agent has greater knowledge on most systems.
    2. The agent should fill in form after thoroughly interviewing the homeowner.
    3. The Agent should advise the seller of his obligations regarding the Property Disclosure Statement and assure timely disclosure.
    4. When listing a new home the agent can have superintendent complete form for builder.

11. Which term describes the lowest wooden framing member of the house?

    1. Pier
    2. Footing
    3. Floor joist
    4. Sill

12. When calculating capital gains on a personal residence, all of the following are true *EXCEPT*?

    1. The cost of adding a 4th bedroom can be added to owner's basis.
    2. An assessment by the city for street lights may be added to the tax basis
    3. An owner may qualify for the universal exemption if the gain does not exceed $250,000
    4. Discount points may be added to the adjusted basis.

13. A buyer is attempting to qualify for a conventional loan to purchase a house. His current income is $4,800 per month and his recurring monthly debt obligations for a student loan and car payment of $500. The anticipated housing expense will be $1,300. Under which rule would be qualify?

    I. Housing 28%
    II. Total Debt 36%

    1. I only
    2. II only
    3. Both
    4. Neither

14. Kelley completes a prelicense class and successfully passes the licensing exam on May 23, 2018. She affiliates with a broker-in-charge and begins working the business as a part-time agent on provisional status. She receives a promotion from her other job that requires her to stop representing buyers and sellers, however continues to refer clients to other agents in return for a referral fee. Which of the following statements is true?

    1. Kelley must continue to be affiliated with a broker-in-charge to keep her license active so that she can receive referral fees.
    2. Kelley is not required to take continuing education so long as she is only receiving referral fees, however must continue to pay the license renewal fee.
    3. Kelley is not required to take postlicensing education by her anniversary date so long as she is only earning referral fees.
    4. Kelley must complete continuing education prior to June 10, 2018 or her license will be placed on inactive status.

15. An appraiser is trying to determine the value of a subject property and has found three similar comps. Using only the information provided what will be the indicated value of the subject property?

Subject	Comp 1	Comp 2	Comp 3
1400 sq. ft.	1300 sq. ft.	1300 sq. ft	1400 sq. ft.
2 bath	2 bath	2 bath	2 bath
2 car garage	1 car garage	2 car garage	1 car garage
$165	Sold $150,000	Sold $160,000	Sold $155,000

10K $50/sq ft

    1. $160,000
    2. $162,500
    3. $159,500
    4. $165,000

16. Which of the following would require a NC Real Estate license according to Commission rules?

    1. A For Sale by Owner who advertises his listing with an online database.
    2. An attorney who is compensated for selling real property at a lien foreclosure sale.
    3. A real estate assistant who holds regular open houses for a listing agent.
    4. An executor who sells estate property and is compensated as a condition of the will.

17. A provisional broker listed a property on 809 Ridge Lane for $425,000 with the seller authorizing both dual and designated agency. During an open house a prospective buyer begins to express significant interest in the property. Which of the following statements is *FALSE*?

    1. The provisional broker should disclose the Working with Real Estate Agents Brochure before obtaining personal or confidential information.
    2. The provisional broker may enter into an oral buyer's agency agreement so long as the potential buyer agrees to dual agency representation.
    3. The provisional broker must disclose all material facts regarding the property no matter the type of agency that the buyer agrees to.
    4. The provisional broker should refer the buyer to another agent of the firm if the buyer desires exclusive representation.

18. All of the following would cause a licensee's license to be on inactive status, EXCEPT?

    1. Provisional broker does not have a Broker-in-Charge.
    2. A broker fails to take his Continuing Education by the appropriate date.
    3. Provisional broker fails to complete 90 hours post-licensing education within 3 years of issuance of license, taking at least 1 per year prior to anniversary.
    4. A broker fails to affiliate with a Broker-in-Charge.

19. Which of the following is NOT a role of the NC Real Estate Commission?

    1. Regulate the activities of Real Estate agents.
    2. Devise a system of education for licensees including continuing education.
    3. To fine agents who have been negligent in their duties and caused damage to their clients.
    4. License individuals and firms who practice real estate brokerage activities.

20. Lily Smith, an agent with ABC Realty, was recently married to John Wilson. Which of the following is TRUE regarding Lily per commission rules?

    1. She may continue to practice as Lily Smith, even if she legally changes her name to Lily Wilson, since most of her clients know her by her maiden name.
    2. Lily has up to 60 days to change her name with NC Real Estate Commission, if she legally changes her name.
    3. If Lily chooses to change her legal name, she should notify the records division within 10 days of name change.
    4. Lily should notify the Commission of her name change at license renewal.

21. Jake Merritt, an agent with ABC Realty, meets a buyer and reviews the Working with Real Estate Agents brochure with him. The buyer listens to the explanation but refuses to sign the acknowledgement. Which of the following is TRUE?

    1. Jake may not work with a buyer who refuses to sign the acknowledgement.
    2. Jake may only work with this buyer as a seller subagent.
    3. Jake may act as an oral buyer agent until he shows a home listed by ABC, at which time he must reduce agency to writing.
    4. Jake may act as an oral buyer agent but he must reduce his agency relationship to writing no later than the Offer to Purchase.

22. All of the following are true of agency contracts, according to the NC Real Estate Commission rule, EXCEPT:

    1. Listing agreement must be in writing from the formation of the relationship.
    2. All agency agreements must be signed by the BIC of the firm.
    3. Exclusive Buyer Agency agreements must have a start and end date.
    4. Property Management Agreements may automatically renew

23. An agent with ABC is on phone duty in her office when she receives a call from an out of state buyer. The buyer has ostensibly called regarding a home that she has seen on Zillow. Which of the following best describes the agent's duties regarding agency disclosure?

    1. The agent cannot represent an out of state buyer and must identify that she works for the seller at initial contact
    2. The agent need only review agency options in North Carolina if the conversation turns to confidential information.
    3. An agent is never obligated to discuss agency options until a face to face meeting occurs.
    4. The agent can only offer Seller subagency to this buyer since the buyer called regarding one of ABC's listings

24. A broker not on provisional status enters into an exclusive buyer agency agreement to assist a friend that is interested in purchasing a home. The buyer has agreed to both dual and designated agency representation. The broker has showed multiple properties, however none have motivated the buyer to make an offer. The buyer inquires about a property that is listed with a broker of the same firm that they would like to see and potentially make an offer. Upon further inquiry of the listing agent it is discovered that the seller has not agreed to dual agency. Which of the following statements is FALSE?

    1. The seller must agree to dual agency before the property can be shown by the broker representing the buyer.
    2. The buyer's and seller's agent will be able to act as designated agents so long as they do not have personal or confidential information about the other party.
    3. In the event that the seller refuses to agree to dual agency, the broker representing the buyer would not be permitted to show the property.
    4. The seller can orally agree to dual agency, however it must be reduced to writing prior to making an offer on the property.

25. A broker receives 3 offers on Sunday on a hot listing in Cary. In what manner should the agent present these offers?

    1. Deliver to the seller in the order in which they were received so that the Seller can respond to each accordingly.
    2. Deliver offers from lowest price to highest price.
    3. Counter each offer and take the first one to accept the terms of the counteroffer.
    4. Deliver offers simultaneously to seller and advise as necessary regarding the merits of each offer.

26. Which of the following is *TRUE* regarding earnest money held in a trust account by a real estate firm?

    1. A cash earnest money deposit must be deposited into the trust account within 3 days of receipt, regardless of the status of offer or contract
    2. An earnest money check must be deposited within 3 days after contract formation
    3. All monies must be deposited within 5 days of receipt
    4. Earnest money must be held by listing agent in their firm's trust account

27. Jeff Pearson, an agent with XYZ Realty, procures a buyer for a home on Sycamore Street. The listing agent is offering a 3% commission plus a $2,000 bonus if the closing takes place by September 30th. Because of repair negotiations, the closing was delayed and ultimately closed on October 2nd. Jeff was incensed, when he learned at closing, that he would not receive the bonus since it did not occur by September 30th. Jeff may pursue all of the following remedies, *EXCEPT*?

    1. File a complaint with the Realtor Association Board of Arbitration
    2. Contact an attorney to discuss possible litigation
    3. Contact his Broker in Charge to determine potential action against listing agent
    4. File a complaint to the North Carolina Real Estate Commission

28. An agent, working as a seller's subagent with Betty Buyer, discovers that there is a defect with the septic system in a house that is the subject of a transaction. All of the inspections and repairs have been completed at this point and there are only a few days before closing. Should the agent inform the buyer of this defect at this point?

    1. No, the agent works for the seller
    2. No, since North Carolina is a caveat emptor state, therefore, no disclosure is required by seller or agent
    3. Yes, since the agent works for the buyer he is obligated to disclose the defect
    4. Yes, since the defect is a material fact, agent must disclose the defect regardless of agency status

29. A broker is representing a tenant under an oral agency agreement while seeking an apartment to rent in downtown Charlotte. The broker has shown multiple apartments, however has not found the right property for the prospective tenant. Over the weekend the prospective tenant attended an open house hosted by an owner that is leasing property "for lease by owner" and entered into a 2-year lease agreement. Is the broker entitled to compensation?

1. No. A broker can only seek compensation offered through a Multiple Listing Service and this property was offered "for lease by owner".
2. No. Since the agreement is non-exclusive, the tenant and landlord are under no obligation to compensate the broker.
3. Yes. The broker earns compensation no matter how the tenant was introduced to the property.
4. Yes. The broker has earned compensation since the buyer entered into a lease agreement, however the tenant must pay the fee, not the property owner.

30. All of the following situations will result in dual agency, *EXCEPT*:

1. A buyer that is represented by the firm decides to purchase a property that is currently listed with the firm.
2. A listing agent that writes up an offer for a buyer that is not working with another broker.
3. A tenant that is represented by the firm decides to rent a property that is currently listed with the firm.
4. An owner of a property represented by the firm under an exclusive property management agreement finds a tenant for a property and the tenant enters a tenant representation agreement.

31. A buyer attended an open house held by the listing agent over the weekend. The buyer calls the listing agent to view the property again because they are considering an offer. Which of the following statements is FALSE regarding this scenario?

1. The broker must explain the Working with Real Estate Agents Brochure prior to showing the house to the buyer.
2. The broker must obtain agreement for dual agency from both the buyer and seller before agreeing to represent the buyer.
3. The broker can provide the prospective buyer with the Comparative Market Analysis that was prepared for the seller if the buyer requests it.
4. The broker is required to disclose all information learned about the buyer to the seller if the buyer elects not to be represented.

32. An agent lists a home and inadvertently represents the square footage as 4,300 square feet in the multiple listing service but disclaims that buyer should confirm if it is important. The actual square footage is 3,400. A buyer contracts on the house believing the living area to be 4,300 square feet but learns of the house's true size when the appraisal is returned. Would a listing agent have liability for this mistake in square footage, given the scenario above?

    1. Yes, agent made a willful misrepresentation
    2. Yes, agent has made a negligent misrepresentation
    3. No, the buyer investigated the square footage as appropriate and there were no damages
    4. No, the agent cannot be held accountable as he is not an appraiser and he disclaimed the representation

33. With regard to Subdivision Street Disclosure requirements, a developer creating a subdivision, not within the city limits, which of the following is true?

    1. An agent, working for the seller (developer), need only disclose the status of the streets , as to public or private maintenance, if asked a direct question
    2. Since 2006, a developer may only create a subdivision with publicly maintained roads
    3. A developer may offer to dedicate the subdivision roads for public use but agent cannot guarantee that DOT will maintain the roads until DOT has accepted roads
    4. Private roads must be maintained by the developer in perpetuity however the cost can be offset by annual fees assessed to each owner by the developer.

34. A provisional broker lists a property for sale in a desirable neighborhood in Durham, NC. The broker receives multiple offers on the property. The seller, desiring the highest possible price for the home instructs the provisional broker to disclose the highest offer to the other buyers. The provisional broker refuses to do so citing License Law and Commission rules that prohibit a broker from disclosing the price or other material terms of a buyer's offer. Is the provisional broker correct?

    1. No. A broker must act in the best interest of his/her client and therefore is permitted to disclose the highest price to seek more competitive bids.
    2. No. A broker is required to follow all lawful instructions and therefore must make the disclosure.
    3. Yes. A broker is never permitted to disclose the price or other material terms of a buyer's offer.
    4. Yes. A broker is not permitted to disclose the price or other material terms of an offer without the express permission of the party making the offer.

35. A broker is representing a buyer that wants to purchase a home, however has recently changed jobs. The lender requires two paystubs from the new employer in order to approve the buyer for financing. The buyer wants to move into a property before school begins and therefore will need to rent for a few months prior to closing. The broker finds a home that the buyer wants to make an offer on. The buyer wants the broker to prepare an Offer to Purchase and a Lease Agreement, with both the offer and lease being contingent of the seller's agreement to both. Which of the following actions is permitted by the agent?

    1. The agent should refer the buyer to an attorney or allow the buyer to make the desired changes in his/her own handwriting.
    2. The broker should add the desired language so long as the client has written an outline of the terms they want included in the offers.
    3. The broker should ask the listing agent to add the specific language to both the offer to purchase and offer to lease.
    4. The broker should prepare an offer to purchase and offer to lease agreement without the language, however add an addendum to both which makes both contingent upon the seller accepting both agreements.

36. A Public Offering Statement for a Time Share development should include all of the following, EXCEPT?

    1. Buyer has a 5 day right of rescission
    2. The date by which buyer may expect amenities such as pool and clubhouse
    3. The buyer's right to have the time share instrument recorded
    4. The developer's obligation to repurchase time share from buyer within 6 months if buyer complains to a regulatory body

37. Which of the following is INCORRECT regarding the North Carolina Homestead Act?

    1. The owner can elect only one property as his/her homestead and seek protection under the act.
    2. The homestead act does not protect the owner from specific liens against the property such as property taxes or a mortgage.
    3. The limit is $35,000, except when the limit is increased to $60,000 for certain individuals 65 or older so long as they meet the legal requirements.
    4. A lien cannot be filed against a property when the unsecured claim is below the Homestead Act threshold.

38. Broker A is representing a buyer that desires to purchase a single family home located in Wake County through an exclusive right to represent the buyer with both dual and designated agency authorized. Broker A is unable to find a property that is listed on the market with the features that the buyer desires. Through a search of public records, Broker A identifies a property that meets the buyer's needs and directly contacts the seller. The seller signs an exclusive right to represent the seller listing agreement with Broker A, authorizing both dual and designated agency. Broker A then writes an offer using the NCAR/NCBA Offer to Purchase and Contract outlining the payment of $500 due diligence and $1,000 earnest money deposit. The offer is accepted and Broker A deposits the earnest money in to the trust account and delivers the due diligence fee to the seller who promptly makes a deposit. The due diligence fee check bounces. What legal remedy is available to the seller?

    1. The contract is terminated under the Good Funds Settlement Act.
    2. The seller must make written demand and provide 1 banking day for the buyer to deliver the funds before terminating the contract.
    3. The offer does not immediately terminate unless the seller elects to once notice is received about the bounced check.
    4. The seller must provide the buyer 14 days to remedy the bounced check before being allowed to terminate the contract.

39. A landlord enters a triple net lease agreement with a commercial tenant for 5 years with an automatic renewal of the lease agreement for 1 year periods after expiration unless either party provides 30 days-notice to terminate. All the following statements are true, *EXCEPT*:

    1. The agreement must be in writing to be enforceable per the North Carolina Statute of Frauds.
    2. A triple net lease is where the landlord takes on responsibilities for certain costs that are typically born by the tenant.
    3. To be protected against 3rd party transfers, the lease should be recorded.
    4. The tenant would not be protected by the North Carolina Rental Agreement Act.

40. Muntin, mullion, casing and sashes are terms defining:

    1. Door construction
    2. Roof construction
    3. Window construction
    4. Wall Construction

1. Answer: 3 - Real property is taxed according to its assessed value, not sale price. The Machinery Act requires that properties be reassessed at least once every 8 years (octennial appraisal). Tax rates can be changed every year and are not set by the Machinery Act, rather by the budget of the municipality.

2. Answer: 2 – The license triggering event is earning compensation on behalf of another. John will require an active real estate license in order to earn compensation from the sale of time share properties.

3. Answer: 1 - Option fee and due diligence fee checks are made payable to the seller and delivered once the contract becomes effective. Offers and contracts must be delivered within 5 days. Earnest money must be deposited the later of 3 banking days from the effective date of the contract or receipt. While it is not recommended that a broker accept cash, it is permitted. When cash is tendered for earnest money or due diligence, it must be deposited immediately but no later than 3 banking days.

4. Answer: 4 – A broker-in-charge must directly supervise provisional brokers. While they are responsible to ensure compliance with agency disclosure and adherence to fair housing, they are not responsible for all violations of license law for a broker.

5. Answer: 2 - Accuracy of all items for the buyer of which he has knowledge. The agent would not be responsible for calculating the seller payoff or aggregate accounting adjustment (set by RESPA).

6. Answer: 1 - The tenant may remove himself from the property and <u>then</u> stop paying rent. Remember that a tenant may never withhold rent while in possession of the property unless there is a court order allowing this or landlord has agreed to this. In addition, a tenant cannot make repairs and seek compensation from the landlord or reduce rental payments by the amount.

7. Answer: 1 - The agent should never draft a provision, even if the client suggests what to write. It is best practice to refer the client to an attorney, however the client can opt to draft the language in their own handwriting.

Practice Exam 1 Answers

8. Answer: 4 - Only the finished basement is heated, finished, and directly accessible from another heated living area of the house. In order for the attic to be included 50% or more would need to be 7 feet, 6 foot 4 inches under ducts and beams; the agent would be able to include area with a height of 5 feet.

9. Answer: 2 - Since the couple were not married prior to purchasing the house, they will own as tenancy in common. Tenants by the Entirety is reserved for a married couple. Joint tenancy is not favored in North Carolina and would require very specific language and instructions be given to an attorney handling the closing. Ownership in severalty is one owner and therefore would not apply.

10. Answer: 3 - Agents should only advise parties of their rights and obligations under the act. Agents should never complete the form for the parties. The property disclosure form is not required for new construction, foreclosure, lease options or transfers among related parties.

11. Answer: 4 – Sill. The sill is the lowest wooden member that rests upon the foundation wall and upon the piers. A pier is a vertical support inside the perimeter of the home used to support the structure. A footing is the foundation wall dug below the frost line. Floor joists are horizontal wooden beams that support the flooring system (subfloor and flooring).

12. Answer: 4 - Discount points are not added to basis. Loan costs would not be added, however capital improvements can be.

13. Answer: 1 - I only
4800 x 28% = 1,344 (could afford up to 1,344 which is greater than payment of 1,300)
4800 x 36% = 1,728 - 500 = 1,288 (not enough since his housing expense is 1,300)

14. Answer: 1 - To be compensated – referral, commission, etc., - a broker must be on active status. A provisional broker must be affiliated with a broker in charge to remain on active status. In order to remain on active status, the broker must renew his/her license by the June 30th deadline, complete the required continuing education and postlicense education.

15. Answer: 4 - $165,000. Comp 3 is just like the subject property except for difference in garages. Looking at comps 1 and 2, you can determine that the difference between a 1-car garage and a two car is 10,000. Comp 1 and 3 are similar except for square footage, therefore the cost per square foot is $50 ($5,000 divide by 100 square foot difference). Then make adjustments to bring the comps in line with the subject.

16. Answer: 3 - An assistant must be licensed to hold open houses for other agents when the property is for sale. Remember that there are different rules for unlicensed assistants performing task under property management.

17. Answer: 4 – Exclusive representation occurs when a firm, through an affiliate broker, represents one party to the transaction. When the firm represents both the buyer and the seller, dual agency occurs so long as both buyer and seller agree. Once a firm is operating under dual agency, when permitted and practiced by the firm, the buyer and seller may be represented under designated dual agency.

18. Answer: 4 - A broker may be affiliated with a BIC or may decide to keep his license active under his own name. If a broker does not have a BIC, the broker may, himself, perform a few tasks such as referrals or representing a buyer so long as they do not hold trust money and the broker has not solicited the business.

19. Answers: 3 - Commission never fines agents. They can reprimand, censure, suspend or revoke a license. The Commission can fine a timeshare developer for failing to register the project with the Commission.

20. Answer: 3 - A licensee must notify the commission upon name or address change, email address, and telephone number whether personal or business within 10 days.

21. Answer: 4 - Oral buyer agency is a legal position to be in until the time of offer (or if agent seeks to exclusively represent the client). In the event a potential buyer or seller refuses to sign the Working with Real Estate Agents Brochure, an agent should note this on the acknowledgement panel and retain it in his/her transaction record file.

22. Answer: 2 - Agency agreements do not have to be signed by BIC. The agent is acting under general agency with a limited ability to bind the firm to agreements with Buyers and Sellers. The others are allowed under rule A.0104

23. Answer: 2 - No requirement to review agency until First Substantial Contact has been reached. The agent will be required to review the Working with Real Estate Agent's brochure if the conversation shifts from facts about the property to personal and confidential information.

24. Answer: 4 – The buyer is represented under an exclusive buyer's agency agreement, which under Commission rules must be in writing. When the buyer's agency agreement is in writing the seller's subsequent authorization of dual agency must be in writing prior to showing the property. Two brokers of the firm are permitted to act as designated agents so long as they do not have personal or confidential information about the other party and one is not a provisional broker while the other is acting as broker-in-charge.

25. Answer: 4 - Deliver offers simultaneously (no later than 5 days from receipt). The listing agent must fulfill his/her duties to the seller by providing advice regarding each offer. The seller will make the ultimate decision on how to respond. An agent cannot accept, reject or counter an offer on his/her own.

26. Answer: 1 - Cash must be deposited within three days of receipt. It sounds correct to say that a check must be deposited within 3 banking days after contract formation, but this is not completely true as it could have been deposited before contract formation or if a check is delivered after the formation of the contract.

27. Answer: 4 - The Real Estate Commission does not arbitrate disputes regarding commissions. The mission of the Commission is to protect consumers from agent's misconduct. In the event of a dispute regarding commission, an agent can file a grievance with the Realtor Association.

28. Answer: 4 - Yes, since it is a material defect. An agent has a duty to disclose material facts to all parties in a transaction. For example, if the agent becomes aware of loan fraud, he/she would be required to disclose this to the lender.

29. Answer: 2 – An oral tenant representation agreement must be non-exclusive and open-ended. Therefore, there is no exclusivity and the tenant is free to look at other properties for lease and not be obligated to utilize the broker under an oral agreement. No compensation is due to the broker.

30. Answer: 2 – A buyer or tenant can choose to remain unrepresented in a transaction to purchase or lease a home. The listing agent is permitted to write up the offer to purchase or lease a property. They do not represent the buyer/tenant and owe honesty, fairness and disclosure of material facts.

31 Answer: 3 – When a buyer/tenant elects not to be represented, the broker owes honesty, fairness and disclosure of material facts. They are not permitted to prepare a CMA for the buyer client or release the one prepared for the seller. They can provide unadjusted sales data to a prospective customer. When acting as a dual agent they can prepare a CMA that is shared with both the buyer and the seller. A broker acting as a dual agent cannot share personal/confidential information from buyer to seller or seller to buyer, unless a material fact, however can share personal/confidential information with all brokers affiliated with the firm.

32. Answer: 2 - Yes, this is likely a negligent misrepresentation. Willful vs Negligent comes down to intent. The agent did not intend to lie. There is no protection provided by the disclaimer other than notifying everyone that they may not have done their job. An agent should never reference commission in a contract and should not disclaim liability. They are responsible for the accuracy of any representation that they make.

33. Answer: 3 - The developer may offer dedication but there is no guarantee of acceptance until NCDOT approves. The roads must be built to NCDOT standards, dedicated and accepted to become publicly maintained roads. An agent must disclose if roads are public or private as this is a material fact.

34. Answer: 4 – Under License Law and Commission rules, a broker is not permitted to disclose the price or other material terms of a parties offer without first obtaining the buyer's express permission. An agent is required to follow lawful instructions; however this is a violation of license law.

35. Answer: 1 – A broker is not permitted to draft legal documents, however is permitted to complete a standard form by filling in the blanks. When a client wants to make a substantial change to the standard offer or seeks to add legal language to a standard offer, the agent should refer the client to an attorney. The client can elect to write the language into the offer, however it is recommended that the agent allow them to do it in the clients own handwriting. The agent is not permitted to write up the language even if the client is giving direction of what they want included.

36. Answer: 4 - Developer has no obligation to repurchase a timeshare based on buyer's complaint. A buyer has 5 days to terminate the purchase of a timeshare. It is important to remember 5 / 5 / 5 / 10 – a timeshare is defined as 5 or more non-consecutive periods over at least 5 years, 5 days to terminate and 10 days for money to remain in the trust or escrow account. Some timeshare agreements allow the owner to stay at the property every-other-year. In this circumstance the timeshare must be for at least 10 years.

37. Answer: 4- The homestead act allows for the protection of a personal residence from unsecured claims up to $35,000, unless an unremarried widow/widower age 65 or older – then the limit is increased to $60,000. There are no protections against secured creditors. The act does not prevent a party from filing a lien, however protects the owner from losing his/her property because of it. The lien holder would not be able to successfully force the owner to repay the debt or risk the forced sale of his/her residence.

38. Answer: 2 – When an earnest money or due diligence fee check bounces, the seller must provide written demand for the funds and allow the buyer 1 banking day to terminate. The Good Funds Settlement Act relates to the closing of the property – where the attorney must perform a final title search, be in possession of all funds and then update title to the property before funds are release. A breaching party has 14 days to delay closing when they are using best efforts to close.

39. Answer: 2 – A net lease is where the tenant takes on some of the costs of ownership typically paid for by the owner such as taxes, insurance or common area maintenance. The NC Statute of frauds requires leases of greater than 3 years to be in writing to be enforceable. The NC Connor Act requires a lease to be recorded to be enforceable against 3rd parties. The RESIDENTIAL Rental Agreement Act does not protect commercial tenants. Individuals/entities that enter commercial transactions as they are expected to be more educated (sophisticated) and therefore there are fewer protections in the Commercial real estate business.

40. Answer: 3 – Muntin, mullions, casing and sashes relate to the window construction. Top rail, bottom rail, hinge and lock stile are all components of door construction. Ceiling joists, rafters, trusses and ridge board are components of roof construction. Sill plate, header, stud and top plate are all components of wall construction.

1. A broker represents a client that invests in commercial property all over the country., that has decided to purchase commercial property in North Carolina. All of the following must be performed in order for the agent to obtain a Limited Non-Resident Commercial License, *EXCEPT*:

   1. The broker must affiliate with a brokerage that is located in North Carolina, serving under a broker-in-charge.
   2. The broker must be a resident in another state or territory with a license in good standing.
   3. The broker must successfully pass the North Carolina real estate exam, however only the state portion.
   4. The broker must notify the Commission through a declaration of affiliation.

2. Which of the following is TRUE regarding the NCBA/NCAR Offer to Purchase and Contract form 2-T?

   1. It is the only form allowed by the NCREC for residential single family homes.
   2. It is appropriate for the purchase of a residential lot in a subdivision.
   3. "Time is of the essence" regarding the closing date.
   4. It allows for a reasonable time beyond settlement date for parties acting in good faith to complete transaction without being in breach.

3. A seller leases a propane tank from a gas company. Per the Offer to Purchase, how will the tank be addressed in the contract?

   1. Tank and contents are considered fixtures and will convey with the property.
   2. Tank is considered personal property of seller and should be entered in personal property section of contract
   3. Tank should be excluded from fixtures provision as it is not owned by seller.
   4. Buyer will be required to purchase tank and contents from seller.

4. Which North Carolina Act requires that attorneys hold trust funds in most residential transactions until the conveyance deed has been recorded?

   1. Good Funds Settlement Act
   2. Residential Rental Agreement Act
   3. RESPA
   4. Regulation Z

5. A provisional broker obtains his license on July 14, 2018. He desires to retain his license on inactive status for the next 3 years. Which of the following is the broker required to do?

   1. Complete continuing education prior to June 10, 2020.
   2. Pay the license renewal fee no later than June 30, 2019.
   3. Complete the Brokerage Relationships Postlicense course by June 10, 2019.
   4. Complete the Brokerage Relationships Postlicense course by July 14, 2019.

6. Per the Tenant Security Deposit which of the following is TRUE?

   1. All security deposits must be kept in a trust account.
   2. Landlords may only collect a maximum of one month's rent as a security deposit on a periodic tenancy.
   3. Security deposits for commercial properties may include reasonable amount for upfitting.
   4. Most residential security deposits should be accounted for within 30 days of termination.

7. Which is TRUE regarding property managers handling of trust accounts?

   1. Property manager must have at least one trust account if he handles trust funds.
   2. Property manager must have trust accounts for each property.
   3. Security deposits and rent monies should never be mixed in a trust account.
   4. Property manager trust accounts may not be interest bearing.

8. Which of the following statements is/are TRUE?

   I. The area under the stairs should be subtracted from the first-floor total square footage.
   II. Square footage in the basement cannot count toward living area unless there are windows on at least 3 walls.

      1. I only
      2. II only
      3. Both I and II
      4. Neither I or II

9. A married couple purchases a home at 1515 Sycamore. Sometime later the husband dies. Both the husband and wife have grown children from previous marriages. How will the husband's estate be settled regarding the home on Sycamore?

    1. Wife gets half and the husband's grown children split the other half.
    2. Wife can express marital interest in the property.
    3. Wife will have life estate in property, children will have remainder interest.
    4. Wife will own home in severalty.

10. When purchasing a vacant lot to build a modular home, a buyer's agent would be prudent to advise all of the following investigations EXCEPT?

    1. Perk test if not on public sewer system.
    2. Review restrictive covenants to assure compliance.
    3. Property survey to determine boundaries
    4. Demographic makeup of a neighborhood

11. A buyer wants to build a home and create an open floor plan, such that the house would be devoid of load bearing walls. What type of roofing system would be most helpful for this?

    1. Rafter
    2. Truss
    3. Hip roof
    4. Gable

12. Which of the following may a homeowner deduct on his income tax return from personal income in regards to his personal residence?

    I. Discount points paid at the time of purchase
    II. Discount points for refinance during the year paid.

    1. I only
    2. II only
    3. Both I and II
    4. Neither I or II

13. A provisional broker is representing a seller of a duplex property located on 202 Nash Street. A prospective buyer contacts the listing agent to set up an appointment to see the home. The provisional broker explains the Working with Real Estate Agents brochure and the prospective buyer elects not to have representation. Which of the following statements is FALSE regarding this transaction?

    1. The prospective buyer is not obligated to sign the Working with Real Estate Agents brochure, however the agent should note the date it was explained.
    2. Upon learning that the buyer is willing to pay more for the home, the provisional broker should not disclose the information to the seller as he/she is acting as a dual agent.
    3. The provisional broker can write up an offer by following the instructions of the prospective buyer.
    4. A legally binding contract will be formed once it is unconditionally accepted and the prospective buyer is informed of the acceptance.

14. A buyer is interested in a home with a $1,245 housing expense. His annual income is $60,000. What is maximum recurring debt the buyer may have and still qualify under the banks ratios of 28/36 if he has other long term monthly debt obligations of $400?

    1. $155
    2. $555
    3. $915
    4. $448

15. An appraiser is valuing a subject property with 1500 square feet, 2 baths, a fireplace and 1-car garage. He has located 3 comps with the following facts:

    Comp one sold for $160,000 three months ago and contains 1550 square feet, 1.5 baths, a fireplace and no garage. Comp 2 sold for $155,000 3 months ago and contains 1425 square feet, 2 baths, no fireplace and a one car garage. Comp 3 sold for $170,000 four months ago and has 1550 square feet, 2.5 bath, a fireplace and a one car garage. Assuming the construction cost are $50 per square feet, the value of a full bath is $2,500 and a half bath is $1,500, a fireplace is $3000 and a single garage is $7,000. The appraiser notes that properties in this area appreciate at 6% per year. What is the indicated value range of the subject property?

    1. $164,075-$169,400
    2. $164,850-$169,200
    3. $164,895-$168,810
    4. $167,900-$168,700

16. Jane owns a large real estate company specializing in the sale and rental of townhomes and condominiums. Sally, who has an inactive provisional broker's license, performs administrative tasks for Jane as a salaried employee. Which of the following statements is TRUE regarding their arrangement?

    1. Sally may show properties for sale or lease since she is a licensee.
    2. Sally may enter listings into the MLS for Jane.
    3. Jane may pay Sally a commission of $150 for each unit that she leases.
    4. Sally must take continuing education classes annually to show rental units.

17. A licensed broker learns confidential information about a buyer, while she is representing the seller. The only way the broker is relieved of the duty to disclose this information to the seller would be if:

    1. The buyer tells the broker that the information must be kept confidential.
    2. The information is deemed to not be material by the broker.
    3. The broker is acting as a dual agent in the transaction.
    4. The broker is acting as a designated agent of the seller in the transaction.

18. Which of the following is TRUE regarding a BIC's responsibilities?

    1. BIC is responsible for all advertisements done in the name of firm, regardless of status of licensee running the ad.
    2. BIC is expected to directly supervise all licensees affiliated with the firm.
    3. BIC may delegate responsibility for trust account to a company financial manager.
    4. The name of the BIC must appear in all ads run in the name of the firm.

19. All the following are true regarding the makeup of the North Carolina Real Estate Commission, *EXCEPT*?

    1. The Commission is made up of 9 members, at least 3 of which must be licensed real estate brokers.
    2. The Chairman is elected by his/her peers for a 3-year term.
    3. The Commission has 7 members appointed by the Governor, 1 appointed by Speaker of House and 1 appointed by Senate Pro-Tempore.
    4. Three members on the Commission are up for appointment/reappointment each year.

20. A licensee fails to pay his fees by June 30th. Which of the following best describes the appropriate step(s) to cure his deficiency?

    1. He must complete current year CE before renewing.
    2. If he discovers nonpayment by Dec 31st for the same year, he needs only pay his balance to begin practicing general brokerage activities.
    3. Agent will pay an increased fee and complete and send broker activation form to Commission by Dec 31st for the same year.
    4. Agent's license has expired and he will be required to complete prelicensing education and pass the state exam if he is interested in continuing to practice.

21. John Simpson has recently removed the provisional status for his license. He is acting as the listing agent for a mini-farm property in Cedar Grove, North Carolina. A buyer calls to ask questions regarding the property and ultimately schedules an appointment to view the property. Which of the following statements is *TRUE*?

    1. John must disclose agency at initial contact with the buyer.
    2. John must disclose agency at first substantial contact with the buyer.
    3. John can only explain agency in a face to face meeting as the buyer must acknowledge receipt of the brochure.
    4. John is not required to explain agency until the buyer requests to write an offer on the property.

22. ABC has a policy of designated agency when dual agency arises. Which of the following is acceptable per NCREC rule?

    I. A PB may be designated for seller but only if a PB is designated for buyer
    II. A BIC can never participate as a designated agent for the seller

    1. I only
    2. II only
    3. Both
    4. Neither

23. An agent, Dan Roscoe, of Wake Realty, is working as an exclusive buyer's agent for Barry Borlen. Barry has not accepted Dan's offer for Dual Agency. Dan locates a house, listed by Wake Realty that meets Barry's needs. Which of the following is TRUE regarding the property?

    1. Dan can only show Barry this house as a seller subagent
    2. Dan may show the Wake Realty listing to Barry as an agent designated for the seller
    3. Dan may act as a dual agent with Barry's oral consent but only if the seller has consented to dual agency as well
    4. Barry and the seller must agree to dual agency in writing before Dan can show the house to Barry as a dual agent

24. A broker on provisional status runs the following advertisement:

    "Most attractive 3 Bedroom, 3 Bathroom townhome in Cottenwood. Close to campus. Own for only $800 per month. Call Chris, ABC Realty, at 919.555.1212, for more details"

    Which of the following is TRUE?

    1. This is a blind ad because it does not contain the name of the Broker in Charge
    2. There is likely a violation of Regulation Z in this ad
    3. "Most attractive" could constitute a misleading opinion as defined by the Unfair and Deceptive Trade Practices Act
    4. This ad has no violations of law or rule

25. An agent receives three offers at an Open House. All the offers are good offers from well-qualified buyers. The listing agent meets with the seller to advise them regarding the offers. Which statement below would best comply with Commission rules and regulations?

    I. The agent, with seller's consent, discloses the terms of each offer to each of the buyers to attract the highest sales price for the seller.
    II. The agent, with seller's consent, informs buyers that they have multiple offers and should present their highest and best offer.

    1. I only
    2. II only
    3. Both
    4. Neither

26. A buyer signs an Exclusive Buyer Agency Agreement with a licensed broker for a period of 6 months. The buyer requests the buyer's agent to seek compensation from the seller, however when none is offered has agreed to pay 2.5% of the gross sales price. Which of the following statements is FALSE with regard to the agreement?

    1. The agreement must be in writing and signed by the buyer with the disclosure of the agent's real estate license number.
    2. The agent will be paid no matter how the buyer is introduced to the property that they purchase.
    3. The buyer's agent must timely inform the buyer that the seller is not offering compensation.
    4. If the buyer becomes interested in a property that is offering a bonus to the agent, disclosure must be made to the buyer at the time the offer is signed.

27. All the following are true regarding a licensee's obligation to retain transaction files, *EXCEPT*?

    1. Files should contain all disclosures given in a transaction for a minimum of three years
    2. A licensee is responsible for his/her own transaction files during the pendency of their transactions
    3. A licensee, who shows 3 homes to a buyer and never sees him again, will not have a file since no transaction ever occurred
    4. If earnest money is disputed and broker ultimately turns funds over to the Clerk of Court, the three-year period will begin to run when earnest money is disbursed to Clerk

28. Dan Phillips, an agent with XYZ, lists a house for $160,000. After a month on the market, with no real interest, he encourages the seller to reduce the price to $155,000. Dan then contracts on the house through his LLC, HomesNTown, for $155,000 with no mention to the seller of his interest in the LLC. Has Dan breached his duties to the seller?

    1. No, since Dan paid the current asking price, the seller suffered no damages
    2. No, this appears to be a good faith negotiation
    3. Yes, by rule, a listing agent can never purchase his own listing
    4. Yes, Dan's action constitute a conflict of interest and seller is entitled to reimbursement of Commission even if there are no actual damages

29. Which of the following statements is FALSE regarding an agent that represents the seller and his/her duty to disclose agency?

    1. When first substantial contact occurs over the phone, the broker must discuss the Working with Real Estate Agents brochure, determine how the buyer will or will not be represented and transmit the written brochure within 3 days.
    2. The broker can represent only one party in a transaction unless permission has been granted by both the buyer and the seller.
    3. When the broker is acting as a seller's agent or subagent that is working with a prospective buyer that is not represented, he/she shall disclose seller's agent status at first substantial contact.
    4. When the broker represents the seller in an auction sale he/she must disclose the Working with Real Estate Agents brochure to prospective buyers bidding on the listed property.

30. A broker on provisional status is working with a buyer client on the purchase of a new home. The builder is offering a $3,000 bonus to agents for procuring a buyer. Per Commission rules, may the builder pay the bonus to the agent directly?

    1. Yes, the commission check must be made to the firm but the bonus check may be made directly to the agent
    2. Yes, but only with the permission of the Broker in Charge
    3. No, only full brokers are eligible to receive bonuses
    4. No, all compensation earned by a broker on provisional status must be paid to a Broker in Charge or Firm

31. Which of the following statements is/are TRUE regarding agency disclosure?

    I.   First substantial contact occurs with a buyer when the conversation shifts from facts about the property to personal information that could weaken the buyer's bargaining position.
    II. The listing agent must disclose his/her status as the agent for the seller at initial contact with the buyer.

    1. I only
    2. II only
    3. Both
    4. Neither

32. A broker-in-charge lists a property located in Asheville, North Carolina for $575,000. A provisional broker is representing a buyer that becomes interested in the property and is ready to make an offer without seeing it. The provisional broker discusses the eagerness of the buyer to make an offer, but both can get the buyer to agree to a showing. Which of the following statements is *TRUE*?

    1. The provisional broker and the broker-in-charge may act as dual agents in the transaction.
    2. The broker-in-charge must appoint a non-provisional broker to represent the buyer.
    3. It was a violation of License Law and Commission Rules for the buyer to be shown the property by the provisional broker.
    4. The provisional broker and the broker-in-charge may act as designated agents in the transaction.

33. A broker has a 25% ownership interest in a property that she has just listed for sale. The broker has not disclosed the ownership interest on the multiple listing service and has not disclosed this to prospective buyers or to the buyer's agent. Is this a violation of License Law?

    1. No. A broker is not obligated to disclose his/her ownership interest in a property unless it exceeds 33.3%.
    2. No. So long as the buyer is represented by an agent that is not affiliated with the same firm as the listing agent, there is no disclosure requirement.
    3. Yes. A broker must disclose the ownership interest to prospective buyers as this is a potential conflict of interest.
    4. Yes. A broker must disclose the ownership interest or violate the Real Estate Settlement Procedures Act regarding kickbacks.

34. Salem Bigg, an agent with City of Oaks Realty, has a buyer client who becomes interested in a For Sale by Owner on Sycamore Street. Salem approaches the seller of the home to ask whether he would be interested in hiring an agent. Seller replies that "yes" he has decided to engage an agent to market the house. Salem takes the listing and promptly assists his buyer in making an offer without disclosing his status as a dual agent. Which of the following is TRUE?

    1. Agent has done nothing wrong if he is acting in "good faith" on behalf of the seller.
    2. Agent is practicing undisclosed dual agency and may face recourse from the Commission and Courts.
    3. Agent can practice designated agency with the "informed consent" of both parties.
    4. Agent could legally be compensated by both parties in the scenario above.

35. Which of the following statements is TRUE regarding Timeshares in North Carolina?

    1. Timeshares in North Carolina are defined as ownership of a property for 10 or more separate time periods over 10 or more separate years
    2. Timeshare salespersons need not be licensed to sell, for compensation, for the developer
    3. Earnest money deposits for Timeshare sale must be held in a trust account for a minimum of 10 days (unless refunded to the buyer prior to this)
    4. A Timeshare developer must be licensed by the NCREC before offering any units for sale

36. Bill Patrick is the Homeowner Association president for Cooley Bluffs subdivision. As president, he is often aware of when neighbors are preparing to sell their homes and move. Bill would like to refer these homeowners to an agent and be compensated when the deals close. Which statement below is most accurate regarding Bill's right to compensation?

    1. Bill may be compensated but only if the compensation is less than $500
    2. Bill may not be paid cash but could receive items of like value in consideration for his help
    3. Bill may not be compensated unless he has an active North Carolina real estate license at the time of the referral
    4. A broker who pays an unlicensed entity for a referral may have his license suspended by the court system

37. Which of the following acts would NOT need to be reported to the North Carolina Real Estate Commission?

    1. A broker that has had disciplinary action taken against another professional license which they hold in addition to his/her real estate license.
    2. A broker that is convicted of embezzling funds from a local non-profit.
    3. A broker that is charged with felony DUI.
    4. A broker that is convicted of felony hit and run.

38. A broker that represents the seller in a transaction is reviewing the closing disclosure. The broker would do all of the following, EXCEPT:

    1. Calculate the commission charged to the seller and confirm accuracy.
    2. Confirm that the property taxes have been prorated correctly between the buyer and the seller.
    3. Calculate the excise tax charge by rounding the sales price to the nearest $500 or $1,000 then dividing by 500 to confirm accuracy.
    4. Confirm the calculation of the aggregate accounting adjustment.

39. A tenant is renting a property for $1,100 per month which includes utilities, however the tenant is responsible for mowing the lawn. During the last mow, the tenant hit a rock which broke the glass in the storm door. Which of the following is the recommended method to repair the glass, which costs $200?

    1. The property manager should deduct the $200 from the tenant's security deposit.
    2. The tenant should pay the $200 for the repair and then reduce the rental payment to the property manager by $200.
    3. The owner of the property should pay the $200 to maintain safe, fit and habitable premises.
    4. The tenant should pay for the $200 repair out their own funds.

40. Which of the following is used to support the foundation, typically made of concrete and is used to prevent settling?

    1. Rafter
    2. Pier
    3. Footing
    4. Sill

1. Answer: 3 – A non-resident commercial broker is not required to the pass the state portion of the licensing exam. They must be a resident of another state, limit themselves to commercial transactions, affiliate with a NC brokerage, not serve as BIC or hold trust money, and send declaration to the commission of the brokerage that they have affiliated with.

2. Answer: 4 - The contract currently allows for a reasonable time beyond the settlement date (14 days) if the parties are acting in good faith. As for the other answers, the Commission does not dictate what form to use, only that it is appropriate. There is a specific form available to Realtors for the purchase of vacant land, so therefore, an agent would not use form 2T. Time is of the essence is in regard to the due diligence date.

3. Answer: 3 - Tank should be excluded from fixtures provision. Had the tank been owned by seller, it would have been considered a fixture.

4. Answer: 1 - Good Funds Settlement Act

5. Answer: 2 – A licensee that desires to retain his/her license on INACTIVE status is only required to pay the license renewal fee each year by June 30th. There are no requirements to take CE or Post education classes. It is important to note that the licensee can elect to take both CE and Post. They may also take Post classes in any order.

6. Answer: 4 - Most security deposits should be accounted for within 30 days. As for the other answers, a landlord has the option to purchase a performance bond and would therefore not be required to place security deposit in a trust account (agents do not have this option). Commercial security deposits are not addressed in Tenant Security Deposits Act (only residential). Maximum security deposits on periodic tenancies are dependent upon term of lease.

7. Answer: 1 – A trust account is not required unless an agent engages in a transaction that requires an account (holding earnest money, property manager, etc.). When an agent handles trust funds, which all property managers do, they must have at least one trust account. A broker would be obligated to have more than one trust account would be if when the broker manages HOAs, in which case, the broker would need a separate trust account for each HOA or if the broker has personal investment properties he/she cannot commingle funds that could belong to him/her.

8. Answer: 4 - Neither is true. An adjustment for stairs is made only when the opening for the stairway is great than the width of the stairs.

Practice Exam 2 Answers

9. Answer: 4 - Since the couple was married when they acquired the home, they held title as tenants in the entirety. Therefore, when the husband died, the wife holds the property in <u>severalty</u>.

10. Answer: 4 - All are valid investigations except the demographic makeup of the neighborhood. It would be a violation of fair housing laws for an agent to advise a demographic study of a residential neighborhood.

11. Answer: 2 - Truss. The trusses are engineered, modular components that allow for lengthy spans and creativity in interior floor plan designs.

12. Answer: 1 - I only. Discount points on a refinance must be spread over the term of the loan.

13. Answer: 2 – The provisional broker is representing the seller and the buyer has elected to have no representation. The broker owes honesty, fairness and disclosure of material facts. Any information, even confidential information, learned about the buyer must be disclosed to the seller once the agent has explained the Working with Real Estate Agents brochure.

A buyer can refuse to sign the WWREA brochure and the agent should document that fact. A broker can write up an offer for an unrepresented buyer, however cannot advocate for the customer as they represent the seller.

14. Answer: 1- $155
Calculate the maximum ratio for total debt: Monthly Income $5,000 X 36% = $1,800
Max $1,800 - $1,245 housing - $400 other long term = $155

15. Answer: 1 - 164,075 - 169,400
<u>Comp 1</u> – Sales price $160,000 – $2,500 sqft + $2,500 F.BA - $1,500 1/2BA + $7,000 garage + $2,400 Appr. = $167,900
<u>Comp 2</u> – Sales price $155,000 + $3,750 sqft + $3,000 FP + $2,325 Appr. = $164,075
<u>Comp 3</u> – Sales price $170,000 - $2,500 sqft - $1,500 1/2BA + $3,400 Appr. = $169,400

16. Answer: 2 - Sally may enter listings into MLS assuming that Jane provided the information to be submitted. While Sally may show properties for lease without an active license, she may not show units for sale. Sally cannot be compensated on a per transaction basis without a license. No CE necessary if agent's license is inactive.

17. Answer: 3 – When a broker represents a seller in a transaction, they have a duty to disclose all information that they learn about the buyer, even if it weakens the buyer's bargaining position, UNLESS the broker is acting under dual agency. Under dual agency a broker cannot pass personal or confidential information with the buyer and seller, unless it rises to the level of material fact. The broker can share personal and confidential information about the buyer and seller with brokers that are affiliated with the firm under dual agency.

18. Answer: 1 - BIC is responsible for all advertisement done in the name of the firm. The problem with the other answers: BIC does not have to supervise brokers (only PBs), BIC may delegate the activity of the trust account but can never delegate the responsibility for supervision. The name of firm must appear in all adds regardless of license status (PB or non-PB).

19. Answer: 2 - All are true statements except "Chairman is elected for a 3 year term." The Chairman is elected/reelected each year. To help recall the composition of the Commission, remember 973211 – 9 members, 7 appointed by the Governor, at least 3 directly involved in real estate, at least 2 non directly involved in real estate, 1 appointed by the speaker of the house and 1 by the senate pro-tem.

20. Answer: 3 - Agent should pay the increased fee <u>and</u> send documents to activate license when expiration up to 6 months. When expiration is more than 6 months up to 2 years, the agent would need to pay increased fee, submit a new background check/application and will be required to either pass the license exam or take 30 hour postlicense class. When a license has expired for more than 2 years the candidate will be treated as if they never held a license and will need to start over beginning with completion of a prelicense course.

21. Answer: 2 – A listing agent must explain agency and his/her agency status at First Substantial Contact with the buyer. A buyer's agent must disclose his/her status as a buyer's agent at Initial Contact with the seller or seller's agent.

22. Answer: 4 - Neither. PB may be designated with any other agent (PB or Broker) as long as the other agent is not his or her broker in charge. BIC can be designated with other brokers.

23. Answer: 4 - Buyer and seller must agree to Dual Agency, in writing before home can be shown to this buyer. The controlling document is the Buyer Agency Agreement. Since the agreement is exclusive, it must be in writing and therefore the agreement with the Seller must be as well.

24. Answer: 2 - $800 per month is a violation of Regulation Z (trigger term, without full disclosure). A broker can advertise general terms such as great financing available or low monthly payments.

25. Answer: 2 – A seller can instruct a broker to disclose the existence of multiple offers to all buyers and give the opportunity for the buyers to bring his/her highest and best offer. A broker must obtain permission from the party making the offer to disclose the price or other material terms contained in the buyer's offer.

26. Answer: 4 – A bonus must be "timely disclosed" which means no later than the point the buyer is considering an offer.

27. Answer: 3 - All are true except "A licensee...will not have a file..." If an agent shows a buyer a home, there will be a file if for no other reason than to keep the Working with Real Estate Agent brochure.

28. Answer: 4 - Yes. This is a conflict of interest.

29. Answer: 4 – A broker is exempt from disclosing the WWREA brochure when representing sellers in an auction sale (so long as they hold an auctioneers license).

30. Answer: 4 - No. Since the agent is a provisional broker, he must be paid through his firm or BIC

31. Answer: 1 – Many licensee candidates mix up first substantial contact with initial contact. First substantial contact occurs with both the buyer and the seller at the point when the agent may learn personal / confidential information about the buyer or seller. It occurs when a buyer asks a broker to show houses or when a seller wants to list. It does not occur when a prospective buyer enters an open house. A listing agent must disclose agency at First Substantial Contact.

Initial Contact – relates to a buyer's agent first coming in contact with a Seller or Seller's agent and immediately disclosing his/her buyer's agency status.

32. Answer: 1 – A provisional broker and a broker-in-charge can act as dual agents – as a dual agent is not supposed to disclose personal & confidential information about the other party unless it rises to the level of material fact. They cannot act as designated agents in the transaction as the BIC supervises the PB and would gain personal and confidential information about the buyer.

33. Answer: 3 – A broker must disclose that they have an ownership interest in a property that they have listed for sale as this is a potential conflict of interest. A broker could not represent the buyer in the purchase of a home that they have an ownership interest it.

34. Answer: 2 - Agent is practicing undisclosed dual agency (without consent from the parties)

35. Answer: 3 - Earnest monies remain in trust account for 10 days before disbursement. Time share ownership is defined as "5 or more separate time periods over 5 or more years". Time share salespersons must be licensed but the time share developers are not required to be.

36. Answer: 3 - Bill may not be compensated in any way (including non-monetary compensation) unless he has a real estate license in good standing

37. Answer: 3 - A broker must disclose convictions, however is not required to disclose a charge. Broker is considered, innocent until proven guilty or if the broker enters a plea.

38. Answer: 4 – A broker not responsible for the full accuracy of the closing disclosure. They are not required to calculate the aggregate accounting adjustment as this is a government set limitation on the amount the bank can hold in the escrow account for taxes and insurance.

39. Answer: 4 – Since the tenant caused the damage, which is above normal wear and tear, then tenant should pay for the repair. The property manager cannot charge expenses against the tenant security deposit until the tenancy ends.

40. Answer: 3 – What is the base of your foundation used to keep you from falling over? – your foot! What is the base of a home's foundation used to support the house and prevent settling? – a footing!! A rafter is part of roof construction. A pier is a support within the perimeter of the foundation walls, often made out of block and is used to support the floor joists. A sill or sill plate is the lowest wooden member that rests upon the foundation wall.

1. Which of the following is/are TRUE regarding agency contracts?

   I. All agency contracts must be in writing from the inception of the agreement.
   II. An agent can disclaim measurements reported in the Multiple Listing Service so long as it is added under the additional provisions section of the listing agreement.

   1. I Only
   2. II Only
   3. Both I and II
   4. Neither I nor II

2. All of the following activities require a license EXCEPT:

   1. Sale of a home that belongs to a family member for compensation.
   2. Managing an apartment building for a friend in return for free rent.
   3. Purchase of a property for a buyer client where buyer pays the commission.
   4. Purchase of an investment property by a Limited Liability Company where seller pays a commission to the LLC.

3. All of the following would be deemed to be a material fact which a licensed agent would need to disclose to a potential buyer regardless of the buyer's status as client or customer, *EXCEPT*:

   1. The previous owner was murdered in the home.
   2. The owner has severed the mineral rights to the property.
   3. The septic system is approved for 3 bedrooms; however, the home contains a 4th room with a closet.
   4. The property was previously clad in synthetic stucco which is an exterior insulation finishing system, however, the owner has had it fully remediated.

4. A licensee is calculating the living area of a 2 story home that includes a bonus room with a sloped ceiling. Which of the following statements is CORRECT regarding the North Carolina Square Footage Guidelines?

   1. An adjustment is always necessary to account for the stairs in a 2 story home.
   2. A licensee can never include square footage where the ceiling height is less than 7 feet.
   3. It is not a requirement that the living area have a cooling system.
   4. A bonus room that is accessed through the garage will be included in the living area.

5. All of the following statements are included in the standard NCAR/ NCBA Offer to Purchase and Contract, *EXCEPT*:

   1. The contract is not assignable without the written permission of all the parties except in the instance of a tax deferred exchange.
   2. The Seller is required to deliver to the Buyer a general warranty deed.
   3. A party that is acting in good faith and with reasonable diligence in preparing for settlement is entitled to delay settlement up to 10 days.
   4. The Buyer may elect to deliver the earnest money deposit 3 days from the effective date of the contract.

6. Sophie James completed all her postlicensing classes thus removing provisional status. She has met the experience requirement by practicing real estate full time for a total of three years. She has decided to open a real estate firm and has decided to operate a sole proprietorship. Sophie asked another licensed broker if a firm license is required and was told that all firms are required to hold a firm license. Is this accurate?

   1. Yes. The Commission requires all firms to have a separate firm license.
   2. Yes. The Commission requires all firms to have a separate firm license and the appointment of a qualifying broker.
   3. No. The Commission only requires a firm license when a firm operates as a corporation or limited liability company.
   4. No. A sole proprietorship is the only form of ownership that would not require a separate firm license.

7. Which of the following is/are CORRECT about designated agency?

   I. It is allowed when the agent does not have personal and confidential information about the other party.
   II. It is not allowed when one agent is provisional and the other agent is a broker.

   1. I only
   2. II only
   3. Both I and II
   4. Neither I nor II

8. Which of following is CORRECT with regards to handling funds in a real estate transaction?

   1. An agent must deliver the earnest money and due diligence payment to their broker-in-charge so that it can be deposited in the trust account according to the Real Estate Commission's guidelines.
   2. The Brokerage is only required to retain the deposit for a timeshare in a trust account for 5 days from the effective date of the contract.
   3. An agent must deliver the earnest money deposit received with an offer to his/her brokerage so that it can be deposited in the trust account within 3 banking days of receipt.
   4. When an agent receives an earnest money deposit in cash it should be deposited into the trust account immediately but no later than 3 banking days from receipt.

9. A non-provisional broker failed to complete their continuing education by the June 10th deadline. Which of the following statements is CORRECT with regard to bringing the license back to active status?

   1. The broker must complete all 3 Postlicensing courses prior to requesting that the license be activated by the Commission.
   2. The broker must complete 8 hours of continuing education in order to request that the license be activated by the Commission.
   3. The broker must cease all brokerage activity on June 11th until they take the general update and 3 elective courses prior to requesting that the license be activated.
   4. The broker must complete the general update and 3 elective courses before they can request for the license to be activated by the Commission.

10. A married couple purchase a property on June 3, 2016 for $475,000 in Asheville North Carolina. There is no mention to how the couple will take title to the property in the standard NCAR / NCBA Offer to Purchase and Contract. How will the couple take title to the property?

    1. Tenancy by the Entirety
    2. Joint Tenancy with the Right of Survivorship
    3. Joint Tenancy without the Right of Survivorship
    4. Tenants in Common

11. The wooden board that is attached to the roof rafters and wall studs is best described as which of the following?

    1. Ridge Board
    2. Sheathing
    3. Flashing
    4. Sill Plate

12. Which of the following are TRUE with regards to the disclosure of a bonus that will be paid to the selling agent by someone other than their principal?

    I.   An agent that represents a buyer must disclose the existence of a bonus to the buyer no later than the time the buyer is considering an offer on the property.
    II. The disclosure can initially be oral however it must be reduced to writing prior to the buyer making an offer to purchase.

    1. I only
    2. II only
    3. Both I and II
    4. Neither I nor II

13. A provisional broker licensee is hired to represent a buyer in the purchase of a property that is listed with another agent within the licensee's office that is not the broker-in-charge. The buyer and seller have authorized both dual and designated agency and the agents are acting as designated agents. Under this scenario which of the following would violate license law and/or Commission rules?

    1. The agent designated for buyer discloses to the buyer that the seller would entertain an offer below the listing price.
    2. The agent designated for seller discloses to the seller that the buyer is preapproved for an amount greater than the list price of the home.
    3. The agent designated for seller discloses that the seller is currently behind on the mortgage payments and that the foreclosure notice should be coming any time now.
    4. The agent designated for buyer discloses to the agent designated for seller that the buyer must sell another home to purchase the seller's property.

14. All the following are responsibilities of the broker-in-charge, *EXCEPT*:

    1. Making sure the firm has a copy of a broker's current pocket card.
    2. Ensuring that all licensees of the firm have completed continuing education.
    3. Ensuring that all licensees of the firm have complied with the Commission's agency disclosure rules.
    4. Direct supervision of all licensees that are affiliated with the firm.

15. A provisional broker is holding an open house for a multi-million-dollar top producing agent. A potential buyer attends the open house and begins to express interest in the property. The provisional broker reviews the Working with Real Estate Agents brochure and the buyer decides that they do not want representation, however still want to purchase the house and ask the provisional broker to write the offer. Which of the following actions would violate the provisional broker's duties to his/her principal?

1. Informing the potential buyer that the owner has received foreclosure notice against the property for sale.
2. Providing the potential buyer with a comparative market analysis outlining a probable sales price range.
3. Disclosing to the seller that the potential buyer would be willing to pay an amount greater than the current offer price.
4. Informing the potential buyer that a highway may be built close to the property line, per NCDOT's expansion plans.

16. Which of the following would trigger first substantial contact, thus requiring disclosure of the Working with Real Estate Agents brochure?

I. A prospective buyer that attends an open house that asks about school systems, square footage, lot size and available financing methods.
II. A prospective buyer that seeks to place a bid on a home being auctioned by a licensed broker / auctioneer.

1. I Only
2. II Only
3. Both I and II
4. Neither I nor II

17. A Provisional Broker who desires to remain on inactive status must do which of the following?

    1. Complete one of the Postlicense classes prior to his/her anniversary date.
    2. Complete continuing education prior to the June 10th deadline.
    3. Pay the renewal fee within the 45-day renewal period.
    4. No action is necessary by the Provisional Broker.

18. A provisional broker enters into an Exclusive Buyer Agency Agreement in order to help a buyer locate a property in Mebane, NC. The buyer locates a property and wants to write an offer. The provisional broker is acting as a designated dual agent in the purchase of the property. Which of the following is *FALSE*?

    1. The provisional broker is permitted to prepare a market analysis for the buyer to assist with determining an appropriate offer price.
    2. The provisional broker is appointed by the broker-in-charge to act as a designated agent in the transaction.
    3. The provisional broker cannot disclose personal or confidential information that they learn about the seller, unless it rises to the level of material fact.
    4. The provisional broker must disclose to the buyer any adverse information that they learn about the property.

19. Which of the following statements regarding lease agreements is/are TRUE?

    I. When a tenant damages a property the property manager can immediately use the security deposit to pay for the repair.
    II. A landlord cannot charge a pet deposit for a service animal.

    1. I only
    2. II only
    3. Both I and II
    4. Neither I nor II

20. All the following statements are true regarding timeshares, *EXCEPT*:

    1. To list or sell timeshares a licensee must obtain a timeshare license.
    2. The initial deposit and fees must be held in a trust account for 10 days from the effective date of the contract unless it is returned to the buyer prior to that date due to cancellation.
    3. Timeshare projects must be registered with the North Carolina Real Estate Commission.
    4. A project broker supervises licensed real estate agents to ensure compliance with Commission rules.

21. Under the 1997 Taxpayer Relief Act all of the following may be added to the basis in order to calculate capital gains *EXCEPT:*

    1. Qualified Closing Costs
    2. Capital Improvements
    3. Special Assessments
    4. Discount Points

22. A broker is representing the buyer in the purchase of a property which is being sold For Sale by Owner. The broker has the seller sign a protection agreement outlining that the broker represents the buyer in the transaction, not the seller and the seller agrees to pay the broker 3% commission. Which of the following would violate license law?

    1. The broker has the seller sign the Working with Real Estate Agents brochure prior to seller signing the protection agreement.
    2. The broker provides the seller with a copy of the protection agreement within 7 days of signing the document.
    3. The broker provides the owner of the property with a sample copy of the NCAR Offer to Purchase and Contract to review.
    4. The broker discloses that the buyer will make an offer contingent upon the sale of their current home.

23. Which of the following is TRUE regarding the members of the North Carolina Real Estate Commission?

    1. The Governor appoints all the members to the Real Estate Commission.
    2. At least 3 members of the Real Estate Commission must not be actively involved in real estate.
    3. At least 3 members of the Real Estate Commission must have a broker's license.
    4. The members of the Real Estate Commission are paid an annual salary that is approved by the General Assembly.

24. Fred Taylor with ABC Realty recently met a prospective buyer. After informal conversations, the buyer states an interest in purchasing a property in the $250,000 price range and begins to disclose his financial information. Per NCREC rule, Fred stops the buyer, reviews the Working with Real Estate Agents (WWREA) brochure. Which of the following statements is TRUE?

    1. If the buyer refuses to sign the WWREA brochure, Fred cannot work as a buyer's agent on his behalf.
    2. Buyer accepts oral buyer agency by completing the acknowledgement section of the WWREA brochure.
    3. Buyer can agree to terms of buyer agency including how he will be represented and the manner of compensation, even though Fred will have only an oral buyer agency agreement.
    4. An agent should always act as a seller subagent until buyer agency has been reduced to writing.

25. A buyer's agent is working under an oral buyer agency agreement. When he prepares to show a property listed by his firm, which of the following statements would apply?

    1. With the buyer's knowledge and consent, they could enter an oral dual agency agreement prior to viewing the house.
    2. The agent must act as a seller's subagent in this situation since dual agency is not reduced to writing and the house is listed with his firm.
    3. Oral dual agency is never legal in NC and the buyer and agent would need to enter written agreement prior to showing the property.
    4. The agent should refer buyer to agent with another firm since all agents in his firm will have the same problem.

26. Which of the following newspaper advertisements by a real estate agent would comply with appropriate rules and laws?

    I. For Sale: 3 Bedroom, 3 Bath Townhouse, available for $135,000. Call John Zimmerman 919.555.1212 for information regarding low down payment financing.
    II. 3 Bedroom, 2 Bath Downtown Condo for sale. Fantastic view of the city from this penthouse suite. Call Chris McKintock, ABC Realty, 919.555.1212

    1. I Only.
    2. II Only.
    3. Both I and II.
    4. Neither I nor II.

27. A newly licensed broker holds an active license on provisional status. The provisional broker begins to send marketing materials to expired listings. Which of the following would not be a permitted under federal or state law or Commission rule?

    1. Mailing postcards to all expired listings in the service area without first obtaining permission from the owner of the property.
    2. Offering to perform a comparative market analysis at a discounted rate of $25 with the permission of his/her broker-in-charge.
    3. Calling a seller directly whose home was listed by an agent of the firm one year after the listing expired when the seller is on the Do Not Call Registry.
    4. Sending solicitation emails once a seller has requested additional information that includes a prominent opt out.

28. Matt Hagan is a provisional broker with Red Carpet Realty. He just listed his first property located at 1802 New York Avenue. The Seller is a licensed contractor that discloses at the listing appointment that the addition on his home was not permitted. The Seller completes the North Carolina Residential Property and Owners' Association Disclosure Statement selecting "No Representation" to all items. Matt is lucky and shows the property to multiple potential buyers but fails to disclose the unpermitted addition. Betty Bryer, one of the buyers Matt showed the property to, decides to make an offer. The home goes under contract and closes in 45 days with Matt never disclosing to the buyer the unpermitted square footage. Which of the following is TRUE?

    1. Matt could be liable for negligent misrepresentation for failing to disclose the unpermitted addition.
    2. Matt could be liable for willful omission if he purposefully did not disclose the unpermitted square footage.
    3. Matt would not be liable to Betty as the Seller should have disclosed the unpermitted addition on the Property Disclosure Statement.
    4. Matt would not be liable to Betty as North Carolina is a caveat emptor state and the buyer is responsible to perform her own due diligence.

29. Broker A submits an offer to Broker B for a property located at 123 Main Street. Broker B reviews the offer with the client who signs the offer with a few minor changes relating to the due diligence period. Broker B texts Broker A stating "We have a deal. Everything has been signed on our side. I will email you a scanned copy in the morning." Which of the following statements is CORRECT?

    1. A legally binding contract will be formed when Broker A receives the email from Broker B.
    2. A legally binding contract was formed when Broker B texted the Seller's acceptance to Broker A.
    3. A legally binding contract has not been formed and Broker B could be guilty of negligent misrepresentation.
    4. A legally binding contract has not been formed because Broker B has not yet emailed the scanned copy of the contract to the broker.

30. According to the NCAR/NCBA Standard Offer to Purchase and Contract, which of the following statements is TRUE once the contract is formed?

    1. The due diligence fee is always nonrefundable.
    2. The due diligence fee is only refundable in the event that the Seller failed to disclose a major repair item in the NC Property Disclosure Statement.
    3. Buyer will receive the earnest money refund only if he terminates the contract by the end of the due diligence period.
    4. The due diligence fee becomes the property of the seller at the time the contract becomes effective.

31. A tenant files a written complaint regarding a nonfunctioning heating system during an extraordinarily cold period in February to the property's management company. The property company is busy with negotiations regarding a new management contract and is running weeks behind in repairs. Which of the following would be a legitimate outcome given the circumstances?

    1. The management company could require that the tenant make the necessary repair.
    2. The tenant may withhold rent until the heating system is repaired in a good and workmanlike manner.
    3. The tenant may be able to move out and receive his security deposit back as well as the difference between his actual rent and fair market rent.
    4. The tenant should have the repair work done, pay for it, and then deduct the expense from his rent.

32. A provisional broker on active status assists a buyer with locating a property that meets all of their needs and promptly goes under contract on June 8, 2018 with closing scheduled on July 1, 2018. The provisional broker completes the general update, however does not take an elective. The provisional broker did pay his license renewal fee prior to the deadline. The provisional broker completed his required continuing education to regain active status on July 3, 2018. The broker-in-charge refused to pay the provisional broker stating that his license was inactive at closing according to Commission rules. Is the broker-in-charge accurate?

    1. No. A broker is entitled to compensation so long as when they earned the compensation his/her license was on active status.
    2. No. A broker-in-charge does not determine when a provisional broker is entitled to compensation, as this is the responsibility of the brokerage owner.
    3. Yes. An active license is required to be paid compensation, both at the time of earning the compensation and when it is paid.
    4. Yes. The broker-in-charge is accurate so long as the required wording has been included in the independent contractor agreement.

33. A couple with $82,000 yearly income is looking to purchase a home with a principal and interest payment of $1,480 per month and yearly property taxes of $4,200 and yearly insurance of $600.

    Using conventional financing ratios what is the maximum non-housing debt the couple can have and still qualify, rounded to the nearest dollar?

    1. $ 400
    2. $ 580
    3. $1,913
    4. $2,460

34. A broker fails to renew his license by June 30, 2018. He decides that wants to bring his license back to active status. Which of the following statements is FALSE?

    1. The broker must pay the increased fee and submit an activation form if they renew by December 31, 2018.
    2. The broker must pay the increased fee, take 8 hours of CE and complete 2 postlicense classes if they submit a new application by July 5, 2020.
    3. The broker must pay the increased fee, submit a new application and background check and complete 1 postlicense class if they seek to renew on March 1, 2019.
    4. The broker cannot earn compensation on behalf of another while his license is expired.

35. The subject property is under contract for $272,000. There are three comparable properties (A, B, C) that sold for $280,000, $270,000, and $295,000 respectively. Comparables A and C had positive features of $5,000 and $17,000 respectively. Comparable B had negative features of $9,000. What is the low value of the probable selling price range rounded to the nearest thousand dollars?

    1. $272,000
    2. $275,000
    3. $278,000
    4. $279,000

36. A broker representing a buyer under an Exclusive Right to Represent, prepared an offer to purchase using the standard NCAR/NCBA form. The seller agreed and the property went under contract. Ten days prior to closing, the city confirmed a $5,000 special assessment for installing city water lines. The listing agent stated that the buyer is responsible to pay the assessment. Is this accurate?

    1. Yes. The assessment is the buyer's responsibility as he/she will benefit most from city water.
    2. Yes. The buyer takes title subject to pending and confirmed assessments per the contract.
    3. No. The seller is obligated to pay confirmed assessments prior to settlement.
    4. No. The seller is obligated to pay pending and confirmed assessments prior to settlement.

37. Per the standard NCAR/NCBA Offer to Purchase and Contract which party is required to pay excise tax and how is it calculated?

    1. The Buyer pays excise tax based upon the sales price of the home, divided by $500 and rounded up.
    2. The Seller pays excise tax based upon the sales price of the home, divided by $500 and rounded up.
    3. The Buyer pays excise tax based upon the loan amount of the home, divided by $500 and rounded up.
    4. The Seller pays excise tax based upon the loan amount of the home, divided by $500 and rounded up.

38. The broker-in-charge supervising a provisional broker states that a licensee is responsible for the full accuracy of the settlement statement. Is the broker-in-charge accurate?

    1. Yes. A broker is responsible for the full accuracy of the settlement statement.
    2. Yes. A provisional broker is responsible for the full accuracy of the settlement statement if the broker-in-charge enacts a policy stating this.
    3. No. A broker is responsible for items that they know or reasonably should have known.
    4. No. The lender and attorney prepare the settlement statement and therefore are fully responsible for the accuracy.

39. Which of the following would *NOT* be the responsibility of a provisional broker handing the sale of a property in a new unapproved subdivision as the listing agent, when the buyer has elected not to have representation?

    1. Providing the buyers with a copy of the signed Mineral and Oil and Gas disclosure in a timely manner.
    2. Providing the buyers a copy Subdivision Street disclosure in a timely manner as the streets will be private.
    3. Disclosing to the buyers that closing cannot occur until final approval of the subdivision.
    4. Advising the buyers about the benefits of taking title to the property as tenancy by the entirety.

40. Which of the following is best defined as the lowest wooden member in home construction?

    1. Ridge Board
    2. Footing
    3. Pier
    4. Sill

1.   **Answer – 4** – Not all agency agreements must be in writing from their inception. The buyer or tenant's agency agreement may be oral so long as it is non-exclusive and open ended (no end date) up until the point that a buyer/tenant wants to make an offer to buy or lease. Licensees cannot disclaim liability – if they report something as true then it must be true or they will be held accountable.

2.   **Answer – 4** – A license is required when compensation is earned on behalf of another (even when compensation is paid by gift card, free rent, meals, etc. or paid by a friend or family member. Exempt activities include those acting as Power of Attorney (or Attorney in Fact) as they are standing in for a party and for legal purposes are that person, representing yourself in the transaction (FSBO / FLBO), or an officer of a corporation or W-2 employee acting on behalf of the entity. Remember the license triggering event is earning compensation on behalf of another. The law applies even when compensation is paid by a friend or family member.

3.   **Answer – 1** – It is not a material fact that an owner died in the property, so a broker would not be liable for failing to disclose it. The remaining items are material facts and must be disclosed regardless of how the buyer is being represented (or not).

4.   **Answer – 3** – <u>H</u>appy <u>F</u>eet <u>D</u>ance <u>A</u>lways – The requirements for including square footage in the living area state that the area must be Heated, Finished and Directly Accessible – as well as 7 feet or more (6' 4" under ducts and beams; unless there is a sloped ceiling where 50% or more must be 7 feet and then you can include where the wall is 5 feet tall). There is no requirement for the area to be cooled, no adjustment for stairs unless the opening for the stairs is larger than the stairs themselves (so you would deduct the open space on the second floor), and square footage that is not directly accessible would be included in other area.

5.   **Answer – 3** – A party that is acting in good faith is entitled to a 14 day delay in closing under the standard NCAR/NCBA Offer to Purchase and Contract. The standard offer does state that the seller will deliver a general warranty deed, that it is not assignable without written permission of all the parties and that the buyer may elect to deliver the earnest money deposit within 3 days from the effective date of the contract.

6.   **Answer – 4** – A sole proprietorship is the only type of ownership that would not require a broker to obtain a separate firm license. Corporations, LLCs and partnerships all require a separate firm license and the appointment of a qualifying broker.

7. **Answer – 1** – In order to practice designated agency the agent cannot have personal or confidential information about the other party. Designated agency cannot be used when one agent is provisional and the other agent is the Broker-in-Charge (BIC). Remember that designated agency allows agents to move back to their traditional advocacy roles. The BIC must supervise the provisional broker and therefore would learn personal and confidential information about the other party. The BIC would either harm their client by not disclosing information that was obtained or harm the other client by disclosing information that he/she became aware of.

8. **Answer – 4** – The due diligence fee is made payable to the Seller and so it does not go into the trust account and should be delivered to the Seller once a legally binding contract is formed. A deposit that is for a timeshare must be retained in the trust account for 10 days from contract acceptance. Earnest money must be deposited within 3 banking days from the effective date of the contract not 3 banking days from receipt.

9. **Answer – 2** – A licensee that desires to keep their license on active status must complete 8 hours of continuing education (unless it is their first renewal) consisting of the mandatory update and an elective unless the licensee is a broker in charge (then they are required to take the Broker-in-Charge Update). When a licensee neglects to take the prior years continuing education they must take the current year (8 hours) and make up the deficiency (8 hours) for a total of 16 hours which will be the mandatory update and 3 elective courses.

10. **Answer – 1** – When no mention is made regarding how a married couple will take ownership to a property, title is taken as Tenants by the Entirety. This provides the married couple with the most protection. Each owns 100% of the property and it will automatically pass to the surviving spouse without having to seek court approval. Joint tenancy is not favored in North Carolina and will be treated as tenants in common unless very specific language is included in the deed.

11. **Answer – 2** – Sheathing is typically plywood or OSB board that is attached to the studs and rafters and the siding or roofing will be attached to it. The ridge board is typically tested as the highest wooden member and is part of the roof construction that is fastened to the ends of the rafters. Flashing is sheet metal that protects buildings from water damage and is commonly found around chimneys. The Sill Plate is commonly tested as the lowest wooden member that rests upon the foundation and is the most commonly missed term on the licensing exam.

12.   **Answer – 3** – Both answers outline the correct timeframe for the latest date, to disclose and reduce to writing, the possibility of a bonus being paid. Note that the bonus can be in cash or some other compensation equivalent – a trip, electronics, gift certificates, etc. The disclosure must be made to all parties if, for example, the agent is offered a trip for 3 closings in a neighborhood, then all buyers must be made aware.

13.   **Answer – 3** – An agent must disclose personal and confidential information about the other party to their client/principal unless they are acting as a dual agent. The fact that a seller is currently behind on the mortgage is not a material fact and therefore does not have to be disclosed. This will become a material fact when the foreclosure notice is posted. An agent is required to disclose material facts to all parties and this would include the inability of a principal to complete a transaction.

14.   **Answer – 4** – A broker-in-charge must directly supervise all provisional brokers. They are responsible for ensuring all agents are in compliance for advertising and disclosure of agency and ensuring transaction files are complete.

15.   **Answer – 2** – The broker is currently acting as sub-agent of the seller, since the buyer has opted to have no representation. Anything learned about the buyer, even if it weakens the buyer's bargaining position must be disclosed to the seller. A broker, regardless of which party they represent – buyer or seller – must disclose material facts. These include highway expansion nearby, foreclosure notice, meth lab, leaking polybutylene pipes, etc.

16.   **Answer – 1** – There is a limited exemption from having to disclose the Working with Real Estate Agents brochure – when a buyer is seeking to make a bid on an auction property.

17.   **Answer – 3** – In order to keep a license on inactive status a licensee must renew their license. Failure to do so will result in the license expiring. There are no Postlicense or continuing education requirements for a license to remain on inactive status. The broker would need to take up to 16-hours of continuing education plus meet the current year's Postlicense requirement plus make up the deficiency.

18.   **Answer – 3** – When a broker is acting as a designated agent they are permitted to advocate for their client. In this situation, the broker subsequently learns information about the seller and must disclose it to the buyer, even though both are represented by the same firm. Do not confuse dual agency (cannot advocate for one over the other) with designated agency (where the agent advocates for his/her client – similar to exclusive representation).

19. **Answer – 2** – A property manager cannot use the security deposit funds until the tenancy ends and then can charge any damage that is above normal wear and tear. It is a violation of Fair Housing to charge a pet deposit for a service animal.

20. **Answer – 1** – There is not a separate license for timeshare sales, just as there is no separate license for Provisional Broker or Broker-in-Charge.

21. **Answer – 4** – Discount points are prepaid interest and therefore may be deducted from ordinary income as an itemized expense, not added to the basis.

22. **Answer – 2** – A broker must deliver instruments (offers, contracts, agency forms) immediately but no later than 5 days.

23. **Answer – 3** – Remember 973211. 9 members of the Commission, 7 appointed by the Governor, At least 3 directly involved in real estate, At least 2 not directly involved in real estate. 1 appointed by the House and 1 by the Senate.

24. **Answer – 3** – While it is ideal to get the acknowledgement signed, it is not required in order to work with/for a buyer. Signing the brochure does not create agency as the WWREA brochure is not a contract.

25. **Answer – 1** – A buyer can orally agree to buyer agency including dual agency representation. Oral dual agency may arise out of oral buyer agency as long as the buyer consents after being appropriately informed of dual agency. It is not necessary to have a written agreement or to refer the buyer to someone else with another firm.

26. **Answer – 2** – The first ad is blind – it does not state the brokerage company which is a violation of license law.

27. **Answer – 2** – A provisional broker cannot be compensated for the preparation of a CMA / BPO. The provisional broker can still earn compensation on the sale of a property. A broker, not on provisional status would be able to be compensated. There are very few regulations about sending regular mail – so no permission is required before sending out marketing material. The listing agreement is with the firm, so an agent of the firm may contact a past client up to 18 months after the agreement expired and not violate the Do Not Call Registry.

28.   **Answer – 2** – When a licensee purposefully fails to disclose a material fact it is considered willful omission. Remember that willful vs. negligent comes down to intent and misrepresentation vs. omission is determined if the agent said something or failed to say something.

29.   **Answer – 3** – If changes are made to an offer then that offer is terminated and a counteroffer has been formed. In order to form a legally binding contract you must have an offer, unconditional acceptance and communication of acceptance to the other party. Receipt of the final documents are not required to form a legally binding contract. A legally binding contract can be formed when an agent witnesses the acceptance of an offer then calls the agent for the other party and informs them of the acceptance.

30.   **Answer – 4**- The due diligence fee is credited to the buyer at closing and belongs to the seller unless the seller breaches the contract in which case it should be refunded to the buyer along with the earnest money deposit and any compensatory costs. The Seller is not obligated to disclose that a property has a major defect as we are a caveat emptor state. The licensee would be required to disclose the item if they know or reasonably should have known about the item. Be careful when a question or answer states always, must, never or only.

31.   **Answer – 3** – Constructive eviction is the failure of the landlord to provide safe, fit and habitable premises. The renter may move out and sue for damages. They do not have the right to unilaterally withhold the rent or to make the repairs and seek reimbursement.

32.   **Answer – 1** – A broker on provisional status or otherwise is entitled to compensation so long as his/her license was on active status at the time the compensation was earned.

33.   **Answer – 2** – First calculate the monthly income - $82,000 / 12 = $6,833. 28% for housing is $1,913. 36% for total debt is $2,460. Subtract from total debt the PITI payment of $1,880 (1,480 + 400 monthly tax and insurance) and you get $580.

34.   **Answer – 2** – When a license has expired for more than 2 years, the licensee must start over by completing a prelicense course, pass the license exam and will be issued a license on provisional status.

35.   **Answer – 2** – Remember that positive features = superior = subtract; negative features = inferior = increase.

    A) $280,000 – less $5,000 = $275,000
    B) $270,000 + plus $9,000 = $279,000
    C) $295,000 – less $17,000 = $278,000

    So the range is $275,000 to $279,000

36.   **Answer – 3** – Per the Standard NCAR/NCBA Offer to Purchase the seller is obligated to pay confirmed assessments where the fees are known through closing. The buyer takes title subject to pending special assessments.

37.   **Answer – 2** – Excise tax is paid by the seller and it is based upon the sales price of the home.

38.   **Answer – 3** – A broker is responsible for verifying the accuracy for items that they know or reasonably should have known and is not responsible for all items listed on the settlement statement. The contract is the best source for verifying the accuracy. In addition, some lenders are refusing to allow the listing agent to see the complete settlement statement (with buyer's side of the transaction). A broker will not be responsible for errors on a settlement statement when the statement has not been provided to him/her.

39.   **Answer – 4** – A broker cannot advise a client or customer how to take title to a property as that would be an unauthorized practice of law. A broker working with an unrepresented buyer, must provide all material facts.

40.   **Answer – 4** – The sill or sill plate is the lowest wooden member. The ridge board is the highest wooden member and part of roof construction. The footing is the base of the foundation installed below the freeze line. The pier supports the home within the perimeter of the foundation walls, often made of concrete block or wood, which support floor joists.

1. Gus is under contract using the standard NCAR/NCBA Offer to Purchase for 1412 Peppertree Lane with the payment of a $1,000 due diligence fee and $1,500 earnest money deposit. The due diligence period expires in 5 days. The buyer has paid for loan application, appraisal, property inspection, survey and pest inspection. Which of the following statements is *FALSE*?

    1. Gus may terminate the contract for any reason and be entitled to a refund of the earnest money deposit.
    2. Gus will be entitled to a refund of the earnest money deposit and due diligence fee if a major foundation issue is discovered and termination is made prior to the expiration of due diligence period.
    3. The owner of the property is not required to negotiate for repairs in the event that a home inspection uncovers an issue that was not disclosed on the required property disclosure statement.
    4. The owner of the property agrees to provide fee simple marketable title transferred by a general warranty deed.

2. A new provisional broker with ABC Realty is holding an open house with the permission of a top producing listing agent in his office. A potential buyer begins to ask questions beyond facts that relate to the property. The provisional broker stops the conversation and explains the Working With Real Estate Agents Brochure. The provisional broker informs the potential buyer that he can act as an exclusive buyer's agent should the buyer be interested in purchasing the property. Is this a CORRECT statement?

    1. Yes, as the seller's agent will exclusively represent the seller's interest and the provisional broker will exclusively represent the buyer's interest.
    2. Yes, so long as the seller's agent is not also the broker-in-charge that is supervising the provisional broker.
    3. No, as the provisional broker may only act as a seller sub-agent in the transaction since he has held the house open.
    4. No, the provisional broker may not act as an exclusive agent since the firm already represents the seller.

3. A non-provisional broker lists a parcel of undeveloped land located in Orange County, NC which is currently zoned for multi-family residential use. The non-provisional broker is aware that the property is about to be rezoned to commercial, which will significantly increase the value of the property. The non-provisional broker does not disclose this to the property owner, rather makes a full price offer indicating that they desire to increase their rental portfolio. Ten months after closing, the rezoning occurs and the non-provisional broker sells the property at a substantial profit. Has the non-provisional broker violated license law?

   1. Yes. It is a violation of license law for a broker to purchase property from his/her client.
   2. Yes. This is a violation of license law as the broker is supposed to act in his/her client's best interest.
   3. No. There is no guarantee that the rezoning will take place and therefore no requirement to disclose.
   4. No. So long as the full listing price is paid by the broker, there is no conflict of interest.

4. Seller's agent A lists a property for sale in a desirable location in Charlotte, NC. Buyer's agent B represents a buyer that becomes interested in the property. At which point must agent B disclose to agent A that they are acting as a buyer's agent in the transaction?

   1. When agent B telephones agent A to schedule a showing appointment.
   2. Prior to showing the home, notice must be provided either orally or in writing.
   3. Once first substantial contact has been reached.
   4. Upon submission of an offer by agent B.

5. A buyer is moving to North Carolina from a state that does not practice caveat emptor. The broker explains that a Seller is only required to disclose material facts that they know or reasonably should have known. Was the broker accurate?

   1. Yes, as the Seller has the most knowledge about the property and therefore must disclose.
   2. Yes, as the Buyer may elect to purchase the property "As-Is" without obtaining an inspection and therefore would not be able to discover material facts.
   3. No, the seller is not required to disclose all material facts, only items required by North Carolina law.
   4. No, the broker should have told the buyer that the seller has no duty to disclose material facts and it is the buyer's duty to discover and disclose.

Practice Exam 4 Questions

6. A provisional broker is working for a buyer under an Exclusive Buyer's Agency Agreement that outlines 3% commission to be paid by the buyer when no compensation is offered from the seller. The provisional broker finds a property listed with a competing real estate firm that the buyer loves. The listing firm has offered 2.5% compensation outlined in the Multiple Listing Service, of which both brokers are members. Upon closing, no compensation was paid to the provisional broker. Which of the following is the best course of action for the provisional broker to take?

1. File a complaint with the North Carolina Real Estate Commission
2. File a complaint with the Multiple Listing Service
3. File a complaint with the local Association of Realtors
4. File a lawsuit against the buyer for the commission

7. Which of the following statements regarding the Standard NCAR / NCBA Offer to Purchase form 2-T is *FALSE*?

1. The seller is not obligated to transfer title free from all liens and encumbrances.
2. The seller is to transfer title under a General Warranty Deed.
3. The buyer is permitted a 14-day delay in settlement.
4. The standard contract is created by the NC Real Estate Commission.

8. CJ owns a property that she is selling For Sale By Owner. CJ is not a licensed real estate agent. All the following are permitted by an unlicensed owner, *EXCEPT*:

1. Payment of 3% commission to the buyer of the house.
2. Offering $2,000 to anyone that refers the buyer that ultimately purchases the home.
3. Payment to a licensed broker to enter the listing into the MLS only.
4. Offering a licensed provisional broker an iPad for referring a buyer that purchases the home.

9. All the following are true regarding time-share sales in North Carolina, *EXCEPT*:

1. The Developer must hold a firm license with a qualifying broker.
2. A project broker must be appointed to supervise brokers selling time-share units.
3. Time-share salesperson must hold an active North Carolina real estate license.
4. The proceeds of sale, including down payment funds must be held in escrow for 10 days following settlement.

10. A broker, not on provisional status, forgets to renew his license, discovering the error eight months after the renewal deadline. His broker-in-charge informs him that he will need to pay an increased fee of $90, with no additional requirements. Is the broker-in-charge CORRECT?

    1. Yes, the only instance the Commission would require the non-provisional broker to meet additional conditions would be an expired license greater than 3 years.
    2. Yes, the only instance the Commission would require the non-provisional broker to meet additional conditions would be an expired license greater than 5 years.
    3. No, when a license expires beyond 6 months but less than 2 years the non-provisional broker will be treated as if they never obtained a license and must meet the new licensure requirements.
    4. No, when a license expires beyond 6 months but less than 2 years the non-provisional broker will be required to submit an application with current background check and will need to meet additional conditions set by the Commission.

11. The listing broker is holding an open house. Which of the following statements made by a prospective buyer would require the listing broker to disclose the Working with Real Estate Agent's brochure?

    I. "I am approved for a maximum purchase price of $250,000"
    II. "The living room is large enough to hold my furniture"

    1. I Only
    2. II Only
    3. Both I and II
    4. Neither I nor II

12. A broker is contacted by a potential buyer to see her listing located at 12 Elm Street. The broker explains the Working with Real Estate Agents brochure and the buyer agrees to buyer agency, authorizing both dual and designated agency. When must the agreement be in writing?

    1. The buyer must enter a written agreement within 3 days from the date oral buyer agency or the agreement will become void and all personal information may be disclosed to the seller.
    2. The buyer agency agreement must be in writing from inception under license law section Agency Agreements and Disclosure.
    3. The buyer must enter a written agency agreement no later than the time that the buyer seeks to make an offer on the property.
    4. The buyer is not required to enter a written agreement unless the seller is not offering compensation and the broker is requiring the buyer to pay.

13. Aiden is representing a seller through an Exclusive Agency Listing Agreement on October 10th. He performed a visual inspection of the property, and viewed the crawl space from the opening noting no material facts for disclosure. Had he thoroughly inspected the crawl space he would have noted water stains on the inside foundation block from standing water that occurs during springtime. The seller made no mention of standing water to Aiden and Aiden did not disclose the standing water to the buyer or buyer's agent. What if anything is Aiden guilty of?

1. Negligent Omission as standing water is material fact that should have been discovered.
2. Negligent Misrepresentation for failure to disclose the material fact.
3. Willful Omission as Aiden failed to investigate the property as required by the Commission.
4. There is no violation as this is a latent defect.

14. A buyer is purchasing a home with a monthly PI payment of $1,450, property taxes of $2,200 for the year and insurance is $800 per year. The bank requires escrowed funds for taxes and insurance. The borrower has recurring debt of $534 per month and the bank uses a 28/36 ratio. What is the minimum yearly income necessary for the borrower to qualify rounded to the nearest $100?

1. $ 6,100
2. $ 6,200
3. $72,900
4. $74,500

15. An appraiser is trying to determine the value of a subject property and has found three similar comps. Using only the information provided what will be the indicated value of the subject property?

Subject	Comp 1	Comp 2	Comp 3
4,100 sq. ft.	3,900 sq. ft.	3,900 sq. ft	4,100 sq. ft.
2 bath	2 bath	2 bath	2 bath
Pond	No Pond	Pond	No Pond
	Sold $450,000	Sold $480,000	Sold $465,000

1. $460,000
2. $465,500
3. $480,500
4. $495,000

16. Annette is purchasing a large tract of land to build a home and farm organic vegetables and raise chickens. The lot does not have access to public water, sewer or cable television. Her buyer agent has obtained a copy of restrictive / protective covenants to review with her. To determine if the lot is suitable for a 4-bedroom house, which of the following should the broker recommend?

    1. Environmental Report performed by Environmental Engineer
    2. Perc (soil suitability) test which may be performed by the county where property is located
    3. The buyer should review the restrictive covenants for required bedrooms
    4. The buyer should obtain a survey defining septic size and location.

17. Broker A is representing a buyer under an Exclusive Buyers Agency Agreement. During team meeting Broker B announces his he has a new listing and that the seller is under pressure with a need to sell quickly. The property meets many of buyer client's needs. The buyer and seller have both agreed to dual and designated agency. Broker A shows the property and writes up an offer, without disclosing the desperation of the seller. Has Broker A violated license law?

    1. Yes, Broker A is acting as an exclusive buyer's agent and therefore must disclose.
    2. Yes, Broker A is acting as a designated agent and therefore must disclose.
    3. No, Broker A, acting as a designated dual agent, can refuse to relay this information deemed confidential which could weaken the seller's position.
    4. No, Broker A and Broker B must act as dual agents since Broker A is aware of personal information that could weaken the seller's bargaining position.

18. The highest wooden member in the construction of a home is best described as which of the following?

    1. Sill Plate
    2. Header
    3. Truss
    4. Ridge Board

19. A buyer is considering the purchase of a property that was used as a gas station 20 years ago. They intend to rehab the building to operate a restaurant. What should the agent recommend to the buyer?

    1. The buyer should contact the Environmental Protection Agency (EPA) to discover potential contamination.
    2. The broker should review public records to determine if a past leak was reported on the property.
    3. The buyer should instruct the closing attorney to review past legal action taken against the property for potential contamination.
    4. The buyer should hire an environmental engineer to perform testing.

20. Charlotte Jones is managing a residential rental property located at 401 Shepherd Lane for Bob Johnson. All the followings statements are accurate regarding renting property in North Carolina, *EXCEPT*?

    1. Should the tenant damage the property during the lease term, Charlotte can pay invoices from the tenant security deposit and the tenant must replace the funds within 30 days.
    2. The owner is not permitted to discriminate against protected classes, even if one unit of the triplex being rented is owner occupied.
    3. Charlotte must hold tenant security deposits in a trust or escrow account.
    4. Should the tenant request repair to be made to ensure the unit is safe, fit and habitable, Charlotte and Bob cannot seek to evict the tenant without cause in retaliation.

21. All the following would be used to determine the gain or loss on the sale of a residential property, *EXCEPT*?

    1. Original Purchase Price
    2. Mortgage Payments
    3. Capital Improvements
    4. Commission Paid on Sale

22. A broker lists a duplex property for sale that is subject to lease agreements. A buyer is interested in purchasing the property to live in one side and have a family member live in the other. Both units are currently rented, one that is month-to-month and the other has 5 months remaining. Under the current situation, the listing broker should advise the potential buyer:

    1. That all lease agreements terminate upon the sale of the property unless agreement is made otherwise between the owner and tenant.
    2. The owner must honor the lease with 5 months remaining, however can automatically terminate the tenancy that is month-to-month.
    3. The new owner may give termination notice to the tenant renting month-to-month, however must honor the lease with 5 months remaining.
    4. The new owner will only be bound by the lease agreements if the seller assigns the agreements at closing.

23. A licensed broker has decided to rent an apartment in a nearby city since a large majority of his residential brokerage sales have been in that area. The owner of the property is not represented by a property manager and is leasing For Lease by Owner. The owner does not have a residential lease agreement and asks the broker to create a lease offer. Can the broker follow this request?

    1. Yes, the broker can use a preprinted form that has been prepared by an attorney.
    2. Yes, so long as the broker has extensive knowledge with regard to property management.
    3. No, a broker is not permitted to write up a lease agreement for the owner to sign under any circumstances since he is a party to the transaction.
    4. No, a broker can only write up a lease agreement when he/she is acting under a property management agreement.

24. The fee paid by the seller, which is levied when any interest in real property is conveyed to another person, is known as a (an)

    1. transfer tax.
    2. machinery tax.
    3. excise tax.
    4. progressive tax.

25. A agrees to sell their house to B, each with exclusive representation by brokers affiliated with different firms, using the Standard NCAR/NCBA Offer to Purchase and Contract for $250,000. The appraisal is performed and is $10,000 less than the agreed purchase price. The buyer and seller agree to reduce the purchase price using the Agreement to Amend Contract. Which of the following statements is FALSE?

    1. Both buyer and seller must sign to amend the contract
    2. The brokers are required to deliver the signed amendment to his/her client within 5 days.
    3. The lender and attorney need a copy of the amendment to perform his/her duties.
    4. Compensation must be paid based on the originally agreed upon purchase price.

26. Which of the following instances would require a brokerage to have multiple trust accounts?

    I. The brokerage holds property management funds (security deposits, repair funds) and earnest money deposits for clients.
    II. The brokerage provides property management services and holds trust funds for rental properties owned by the brokerage.

    1. I Only
    2. II Only
    3. Both I and II
    4. Neither I nor II

27. A seller lists his property for sale with Zippy Realty under an Exclusive Right to Sell listing agreement. The seller is concerned about conflicts of interest and does not initially agree to dual agency representation. Two weeks have passed since listing the home and while there have been multiple showings no offers have been received. A buyer that is represented by a provisional broker with Zippy Realty is interested in viewing the home. The listing broker asks the seller to consent to dual and designated agency representation. Which of the following is FALSE?

    1. The seller is not obligated to consent to dual/designated agency, however the buyer's agent would not be permitted to show the listing as a buyer's agent.
    2. The seller may orally agree to dual and designated agency, subsequent to listing the property and it may be oral if the buyer agency agreement is oral.
    3. Should the buyer desire to view the home and be represented, the buyer agency agreement must be terminated and buyer referred to another brokerage company since no change may be sought in a representation once agreed to in writing.
    4. Should the seller consent to dual and designated agency, the buyer and seller agents may act as dual agents in the event that the listing agent is not also the supervising broker-in-charge.

28. A new provisional broker obtains his/her real estate license on August 3, 2018. All the following are correct regarding maintaining a license on active status, *EXCEPT*?

    1. Completion of 8 hours of continuing education by June 10, 2019
    2. Payment of the license renewal fee by June 30, 2019.
    3. Completion of at least one postlicense course by August 3, 2019
    4. Affiliation with a supervising broker-in-charge.

29. Which of the following advertisements placed by licensed brokers would comply with License Law and Commission Rules?

    I. Large 3 bedroom 2 bath home in desirable neighborhood for only $215,000. Call Anita James at 919-555-1212.
    II. You either fulfill your dreams or someone else. Great opportunity to own investment property while your tenant pays the mortgage. One unit rents for $1,400. Large duplex for only $280,000. Call James Jones, Broker XYZ Realty at 919-555-1212.

    1. I only
    2. II only
    3. Both
    4. Neither

30. All the following statements regarding real property taxation in North Carolina are true, EXCEPT:

    1. Property taxes are charged to buildings, structures and land based upon the assessed value.
    2. A manufactured home will always be charged real property taxes based upon the assessed value.
    3. The assessed value for the property may change every year, but must be adjusted every eight years.
    4. The assessed value does not change to the sales price when a property is sold, rather changes during a revaluation year.

31. A broker is working with a buyer as a seller's subagent in the purchase of a resale property that is located outside the city limits built in 1998. The roads in the subdivision are deteriorating and the buyer asks if roads are publicly or privately maintained. The broker informs the buyer that for all subdivisions built after October 1, 1975 the subdivision builders must establish a fund for road maintenance when roads are private and that private roads must be marked as private on the sign. What if anything is the agent guilty of?

    1. Willful Omission
    2. Negligent Omission
    3. Negligent Misrepresentation
    4. Willful Misrepresentation

32. Both the buyer and seller have exclusive representation by provisional brokers under respective buyer agency and listing agreements. The listing firm has offered 3.5% commission to be paid to the selling agent. Upon closing, the listing firm pays both the buyer and seller agent his/her compensation directly. Does this violate license law?

    1. Yes, compensation cannot be paid directly to the buyer agent.
    2. Yes, neither buyer or sellers agent may be paid directly.
    3. No, it is common practice for the listing firm to pay agents compensation directly to the agent that earned the commission.
    4. No, the Real Estate Commission does not set rules regarding payment of compensation to provisional brokers.

33. An agent is working with a buyer in the purchase of a property located in a subdivision that has experienced well and septic issues. Recently the city has decided to extend service to the subdivision, which will substantially increase the value of the home. The agent fails to disclose this fact to the seller, however does disclose this to the buyer. Has the agent acted properly?

    1. Yes, as the agent's fiduciary duties including loyalty are with the buyer and it would weaken his/her bargaining position.
    2. Yes, as it is the duty of the seller to protect his/her interest by remaining informed about changes that may impact the value of the property.
    3. No, the agent has a duty to disclose material facts relating to the property to both parties regardless of the party that is represented.
    4. No, the agent represents the seller and owes loyalty to the seller only.

34. A broker has completed all 3 postlicense classes since obtaining his/her license two years ago. They have decided to open a firm to represent clients in the purchase and sale of residential homes. All of the following would be required to elect to be broker-in-charge of the new company, *EXCEPT*:

    1. 2 years full time experience as a non-provisional broker.
    2. Active license in good standing.
    3. Election form sent to the Commission.
    4. Completion of the 12-hour Broker-in-Charge course within 120 days of becoming broker-in charge.

35. A commercial broker actively licensed in good standing in a state other than North Carolina is interested in representing buyers and sellers in the sale or lease of commercial property. Which of the following would NOT be required in order for the agent to lawfully engage in this type of brokerage activity?

    1. Broker must pass the State portion of the licensure exam.
    2. Affiliate with a brokerage that is licensed in North Carolina.
    3. Limit activity solely to commercial transaction, however may earn referral fees for residential transactions.
    4. Apply for limited license, including a background check.

36. During a continuing education class a student asks if a referral fee may be paid to a broker that is on active status, however is not affiliated with a broker-in charge. The instructor states that this is permitted and in addition highlights that compensation cannot be paid to a licensee that is on inactive status. Is the instructor's response CORRECT?

    1. Yes, as a licensee is always permitted to receive referral fees.
    2. Yes, as a broker that has removed provisional status may be on active status even though they are not affiliated with a BIC or obtained BIC status.
    3. No, in order for a broker to be on active status, they must be affiliated with a BIC or obtain BIC status.
    4. No, as payment of referral fees are a violation of RESPA rules regarding compensation to third parties.

37. Bruce represents a buyer that is under contract to purchase a property listed with Suzette, another broker of his firm. A local closing attorney is handling the settlement and closing of the property. Which of the following statements is TRUE regarding settlement and closing?

    1. Bruce and Suzette are not permitted to represent both parties at closing and must refer each to an attorney.
    2. The seller must pay the commission after all parties have signed the required documents.
    3. The settlement agent cannot release funds until all funds have been received from the buyer, lender or others and the deed and deed of trust have been recorded.
    4. Bruce and Suzette are responsible for the accuracy of the entire closing statement and can be found liable if a mistake is not discovered.

38. Russell is preparing to list a single-family property in Chapel Hill, North Carolina. The local multiple listing service requires Russell to report the living area of the property. Which of the following statements is FALSE regarding Commission guidelines for square footage?

    1. Russell must be reasonably accurate when disclosing square footage.
    2. The buyer's agent must verify the accuracy of Russell's calculation by measuring the home.
    3. Russell should compare his calculation with tax records to identify potential issues.
    4. The living area must be heated, finished and directly accessible.

39. Which of the following statements regarding home construction is/are CORRECT?

    I. Muntin, mullion, sill and sash are components of a window.
    II. The footing is the lowest point of construction, below the foundation wall.

    1. I Only
    2. II Only
    3. Both I and II
    4. Neither I nor II

40. Which of the following is NOT the responsibility of a Broker-in-Charge?

    1. The Broker-in-Charge is responsible for any violation of license law by a provisional or non-provisional broker that is affiliated with the firm.
    2. The Broker-in-Charge must review all ads placed by provisional and non-provisional brokers.
    3. The Broker-in-Charge must ensure that earnest money that is paid by check is deposited the later of 3 banking days following the receipt of funds or the effective date of contract.
    4. The Broker-in-Charge must ensure that transactions records are retained for at least 3 years from the date of last activity.

1. Answer: 2 - The due diligence fee is credited when the buyer purchases the property or is refunded if the seller breaches the contract. Due diligence is similar to an option– where the buyer can purchase or terminate the contract for any reason or no reason. The seller is not required to negotiate repairs. The owner agrees to provide a general warranty deed and fee simple marketable title.

2. Answer: 4 – Should the potential buyer elect to purchase the property and hire the provisional broker to represent them, dual agency would arise (both buyer and seller represented by the same firm). The provisional broker can represent the buyer under dual or designated dual agency (so long as he/she does not have personal and confidential information about the seller, and is not designated against the BIC). The potential buyer could also elect to be unrepresented.

3. Answer: 2 – License law prohibits "self-dealing". It is the duty of the broker to put the clients interest above his/her own interest. A broker cannot secretly profit from a property where he/she is supposed to be representing the client.

4. Answer: 1 – The buyer's agent must disclose his / her status to the seller or seller's agent at initial contact. This often occurs over the phone when scheduling an appointment, however may occur all the way up to presenting an offer. The first time the buyer's agent interacts with the seller or seller's agent, they must disclose that they represent the buyer. It allows each party to protect information about his/her client.

5. Answer: 3 – In North Carolina the seller has limited items where they are mandated to disclose information regarding the house. There are some items that are deemed material facts by the real estate commission, so the seller must disclose synthetic stucco (EIFS – Exterior Insulating Finishing System) when the home is clad or has been previously clad and replaced, leaking polybutylene pipes and if the property has ever been the site of a methamphetamine lab. In addition a seller must disclose if they severed or plan to sever oil, mineral or gas rights. The seller can select NO REPRESENTATION on the Residential Property Owner Association Disclosure Statement. It is the duty of the buyer to perform inspections on the property and the agents to disclose material facts known or those they reasonably should have known. Selling a property "As-Is" does not relieve the brokers from disclosing material facts.

6. Answer: 3 – The NC Real Estate Commission will not hear complaints regarding compensation – regarding the amount or non-payment. The Multiple Listing service also will not hear complaints regarding commission. The Association of Realtors will hear complaints/grievances including disputes regarding commission. While the broker may sue the buyer for the commission in certain circumstances, it is not the best course of action.

7. Answer: 4 – The Commission does not create contract forms, the NCAR does. The Commission sets the rules for standard forms and the brokerage will determine if association forms will be used or hire an attorney to create standard forms for the office. It is important to know the definition of an encumbrance. It is a common mistake to think only of financial liens as encumbrances – however encroachments, easements, deed restrictions and restrictive/protective covenants are also encumbrances. Most of these items, excluding encroachments which may be cured, run with the land and the seller would not, on his/her own, terminate them.

8. Answer: 2 – The requirement for obtaining a real estate license is earning compensation on behalf of another. A buyer, who is party to the transaction, may be paid compensation, however it must be disclosed to the lender and included on the settlement statement. It is illegal, even for the owner of a property, to offer compensation to an unlicensed individual for referring a buyer. Compensation can be money, gift cards, travel and non-cash items such as iPads.

9. Answer: 1 – The developer must register the time share project with the Commission, however is not required to obtain a firm license. The remaining items are true. It is important to remember 5/5/5/10 – a time share must have 5 separate time periods, over at least 5 years, the buyer has 5 days from purchase to cancel and the funds from sale must be held in escrow for at least 10 days, unless buyer terminates.

10. Answer: 4 – When a license has expired for more than 6 months, the Commission will require payment of the increased fee ($90), application and updated background check. The Commission will require brokers that were not provisional to take postlicense class(es) or sit for the licensure exam as a penalty. An individual whose license has been expired for more than 5 years will be treated as if they never obtained a license. The 3-year requirement relates to active licenses that need to complete postlicense courses – one per year prior to his/her anniversary date.

11. Answer: 1 – The requirement to disclose the Working with Real Estate Agent's brochure is at first substantial contact, the point that the conversation is shifting from facts about the property to personal / confidential information that could weaken a party's bargaining position. Disclosing the maximum price a buyer is willing to pay, the amount a lender has approved a buyer for, a buyer's special interest in this particular property, etc. is considered first substantial contact. The statement that a room is large, relates to the property itself.

12. Answer: 3 – All agreements eventually need to be in writing, however in certain circumstances a client may orally agree to representation. As a rule, agreements to list a property for sale or for lease are required to be in writing from inception. Agreements with buyers or tenants are permitted to be oral so long as they are not exclusive and provide for no end date. Oral agreements must be reduced to writing prior to a party making an offer to sell or lease the property.

13. Answer: 4 – An agent is responsible for disclosing facts that they know or reasonably should have known. Since Aiden performed a visual inspection of the property with no noted defects, he would not be liable. The defect is a latent defect – meaning hidden. Brokers are not required to visually inspect the entire crawlspace or to discover concealed problems. Had the seller disclosed the issue, then Aiden would be required to disclose as a material fact, even if standing water is not present at the current time. Willful vs. Negligent comes down to intent or a broker's failure to take additional action when informed about a material fact. Omission vs. Misrepresentation comes down to the broker not saying something or saying something that was untrue.

14. Answer: 4 – It is important to read the question to see if the problem is asking for monthly or yearly income to qualify. The first step is to add up the monthly housing payment (Principal, Interest, Taxes and Insurance), or $1,700 (1,450 PI + 250 TI). Next calculate total debt by adding the housing payment to long term debt, or $2,234 (1,700 + 534). Divide the housing payment of $1,700 by 28% to get a minimum monthly income of $6,071 and minimum yearly of $72,857. Next take the monthly total debt payment of $2,234 and divide by 36% to get a minimum monthly income of $6,205 and yearly income of $74,466. The minimum yearly income will be the higher of the 2 or $74,466. Now round it to the nearest $100 = $74,500.

15. Answer: D - $495,000

Subject	Comp 1 - $450,000	Comp 2 - $480,000	Comp 3 - $465,000
4,100	3,900 – add 15,000	3,900 – add 15,000	4,100 – No ADJ
Pond	No Pond– add 30,000	Pond – No ADJ	No Pond – add 30,000
	$495,000	$495,000	$495,000

16. Answer: 2 – A property that does not have access to a public sewer system will require a septic system. To determine the type of system or if the soil will not be suitable – a buyer would obtain a perc test. This test can be performed by a private company (if allowed by local regulations) or will be performed by the county. An environmental engineer is used to determine if soil has been contaminated. Covenants are important for minimum construction standards, however not the best choice for determining soil suitability. A survey details locations of items on the property, however does not include soil testing.

17. Answer: 4 – When a firm represents both the buyer and seller in a transaction dual agency arises. Next it must be determined if the buyer or seller's agent can act as designated agents. The firm must practice designated agency and both the buyer and sell must agree. Designated agency cannot be practiced if one broker is a PB and the other broker is the BIC or if either agent has personal / confidential information about the other party. In this instance, the agent that represents the buyer learned confidential information in the team meeting. Neither agent will be permitted to designate, and therefore the broker did not violate license law by not disclosing personal / confidential information about the seller.

18. Answer: 4 – Of the choices provided, the ridge board is the highest wooden member (roof sheathing if provided as an option would be higher). The sill or sill plate is the lowest wooden member that rests upon the foundation wall and top of the piers. A header is additional horizontal support over doors, windows and open spans. Trusses are used in roof construction and allow for fewer load bearing walls and open floor plans.

19. Answer: 4 – When a buyer is purchasing property that may have been environmentally contaminated, a broker should recommend the use of an Environmental Engineer (to assess potential risk/contamination). The EPA can provide information and will investigate reports of active contamination, it is not the best recommendation. The attorney is not responsible for assisting the buyer to determine contamination. The public record may not contain information regarding contamination, as it has not been discovered.

20. Answer: 1 – A property manager/ owner cannot access the tenant security deposit until the end of the tenancy where tenant has vacated. There are permitted uses and limits on the amount that can be charged according to the Tenant Security Deposit Act. When an owner hires a licensed broker, they lose the limited exemptions that they may have to discriminate. Security deposits must be held in a trust account when a licensee is involved (even personally owned by the broker), or if unlicensed – the landlord may be bonded. The property manager and owner are not permitted to retaliatory eviction when a tenant exerts his/her right to habitable premises. The owner/property manager would not be required to renew a lease upon expiration of the initial lease term.

21. Answer: 2 – Mortgage payments do not impact the gain or loss on a property, however will be used to determine equity if they include payments to principal. The remainder are factors used to determine basis or the amount realized in the sale of a property.

22. Answer: 3 – Lease agreements do not terminate upon sale of the property and therefore must be honored by the new owner. Assignment should take place at closing, however failure to do so will not invalidate the existing lease agreements.

23. Answer: 1 – If you restate the question to its base form, it would be "can a broker complete an offer to purchase/lease a property when it is for his/her own use?" When you get a real estate license it does not mean that you can never represent yourself. A broker can make offers for sales or leases on preprinted forms or elect to write his/her offer on a bar napkin for that matter. It is recommended to use preprinted forms written by an attorney for the protection of all parties. The broker should understand lease agreements, however is not required to be knowledgeable in property management as he is a tenant.

24. Answer: 3 – Excise tax, formerly known as revenue stamps is a state tax charged at a rate of $1 per $500 of sales price, or any fraction thereof (sales price / $500, round up). The county collects the taxes and remits them to the State.

25. Answer: 4 – Commission is typically paid as a percentage of the sales price unless the agreement states otherwise. In order to change the terms of a contract, agreement must be made in writing and signed by all parties. Brokers are required to deliver documents immediately but no later than 5 days which include offers, contracts, amendments, etc. When changes are made to a contract, especially when it relates to purchase price, the lender and attorney will need to be provided a copy.

26. Answer: 2 – Trust account money, "other people's money", cannot comingle with money that is /or may belong to the firm. In option I, all of the funds belong to clients, not the firm. In option II, the firm has an interest in the security deposits and repair funds of its tenants and therefore would be required to have an additional trust account. They must keep other people's money separate from funds that they have an interest in.

27. Answer: 3 – The seller may be asked to amend the listing contract to authorize dual and/or designated dual agency. The determination about whether it must be in writing or is permitted to be oral is the status of the buyer agency agreement. When the buyer agency agreement is written, the change by the seller must be in writing. When the buyer agency agreement is oral, the change by the seller may be oral up until the buyer decides to make an offer to purchase.

28. Answer: 1 – A newly licensed broker does not have to take continuing education prior to the first renewal, however would need to meet the 8 hour requirement in subsequent years to remain on active status. In this instance the broker would need to complete CE by June 10, 2020.

29. Answer: 2 – The first advertisement is a "blind ad" where it is not apparent that Anita has a real estate license and is selling a home for another. The second, while listing disclosing numbers such as the rental amount would comply.

30. Answer: 2 – Manufactured homes are considered personal property and taxed like cars until it becomes real property – wheels and hitch removed, placed on a permanent foundation on land that is owned or leased for at least 20 years. The assessed value for property may change every year but must change at least every 8 years (octennial reappraisal). The assessed value in North Carolina does not change to the sales price when a property is sold.

31. Answer: 3 – A broker must investigate to determine if roads are public or privately maintained as this is a material fact. When a property is initially sold by a developer, after October 1, 1975, the developer must disclose if roads are public or private by providing the Subdivision Street Disclosure Statement. Willful vs. Negligent is determined by intent, and the facts of the question fail to show intent. Misrepresentation vs. Omission is determined by the agent stating something or remaining silent. In this case the agent made a representation and was wrong.

32. Answer: 1 – Commission to a provisional broker can only be paid through his or her brokerage. Compensation cannot be paid directly by any other party. The buyer's agent does not work for the listing brokerage since both clients are represented under exclusive agency.

33. Answer: 3 – A broker owes disclosure of material facts to all parties regardless of agency status (representing the buyer, seller or both). In this transaction the agent is acting as seller subagent, since the question states the agent is working "with a buyer". While it does not impact the answer, it is important to watch out for working "with" (customer) or working "for" (client).

34. Answer: 1 – The broker must have 2 years full time experience or the equivalent over a 5 year period when working part-time. The clock starts when the broker obtains a license and actively is engaged in the business, not when he/she removes provisional status.

35. Answer: 1 – A broker seeking a Limited Non-Resident Commercial License does not need to pass the State portion of the licensing exam. They must meet the other requirements. In addition, they are not permitted to hold trust funds as they must be delivered to the NC firm they have affiliated with.

36. Answer: 2 – There is a limited area where a non-provisional broker can hold an active license and not be affiliated with BIC or acting as BIC. The limits are severe – as a broker must be BIC or affiliated with a BIC in order to solicit business, advertise, use yard signs, handle trust money and limits on other brokers joining the firm. RESPA relates to payment by third parties such as lenders, inspectors, insurance agents, etc.

37. Answer: 3 - Under the Goods Funds Settlement Act, the settlement agent must ensure that all funds have been received from the buyer, lender and others (seller, etc.) and ensure that the deed and deed(s) of trust have been recorded before closing is completed and funds are released. A broker will not receive commission, seller proceeds will not be released and keys will not change hands until closing has occurred as defined above. Brokers are not responsible for the entire accuracy of the settlement statement (also called closing disclosure when lender financing is involved). They are responsible for what they know or reasonably should have known. A broker is not required to recalculate the mortgage payoff or aggregate accounting adjustment. The contract is the best resource for determining the accuracy of the settlement statement.

38. Answer: 2 – A buyer's agent can rely on the listing agent's square footage calculation unless it is apparent that it is wrong. The buyer's agent should compare the square footage reported to tax records to determine potential issues. The buyer's agent is responsible for failing to discover an error when a reasonably prudent agent would have discovered the issues. The Commission does not require the disclosure of square footage, however when reported it must be accurate. In general, unless material, an agent has a 5% tolerance up or down when an error is made calculating the square footage.

39. Answer: 3 – A window is comprised of muntins, mullions, sills and sashes. The footing is the base of the foundation of a home, just as the foot is the base of your foundation (the lowest point of your body).

40. Answer: 1 – The BIC is responsible for the actions of provisional brokers that they supervise. They are not responsible for all actions of non-provisional brokers unless the violation is for advertising or agency disclosure.

Additional Study Resources
Available on our Website:

www.3WiseTeachers.com/forms

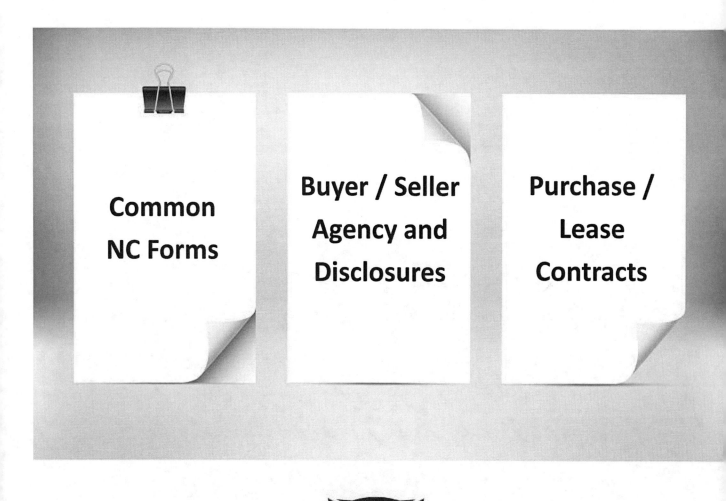

Common NC Forms

Buyer / Seller Agency and Disclosures

Purchase / Lease Contracts

3 Wise Teachers

Check out our other products at:

www.3WiseTeachers.com

New exam products coming soon!!

Available Now

Real Estate Prelicense

Math Workbook

Matt Davies
Doug Sinclair
Tiffany Stiles

Second Edition

North Carolina
Real Estate Educators
2017
Program Of The Year

Available Now

National Real Estate

Exam Review

Matt Davies
Tiffany Stiles

Update Edition

3 Wise Teachers